excellence in
Supply Chain
Management

How to understand and improve supply chains

Contents

About the Book

In writing this book, I have made best-efforts endeavours not to include anything that, if used, would be injurious or cause financial loss to the user. The user is, however, strongly recommended, before applying or using any of the contents, to check and verify their own company policy/requirements. No liability will be accepted by the author for the use of any of the contents.

It can also happen in a lifetime of learning and meeting people, that the original source of an idea or information has been forgotten. If I have actually omitted in this book to give anyone credit they are due, I apologise and hope they will make contact so I can correct the omission in future editions.

Included at the end of each part of this book, are "Action Times". These exercises are here so that students and others may practise their application skills.

About the Author

Stuart Emmett

My own journey to "today", whilst an individual one, does not happen, thankfully, without other people's involvement. I smile when I remember so many helpful people. So to anyone who has ever had contact with me, then please be assured you will have contributed to my own learning, growing and developing.

After spending over 30 years in commercial private sector service industries, working in the UK and in Nigeria, I then moved into Training. This was associated with the, then, Institute of Logistics and Distribution Management (now the Chartered Institute of Logistics and Transport).

After being a Director of Training for nine years, I then choose to become a freelance independent mentor/coach, trainer and consultant. This built on my past operational and strategic experience and my particular interest in the "people issues" of management processes. Trading under the name of Learn and Change Limited, I now enjoy working on five continents, principally in Africa and the Middle East, but also in the Far East, Europe and South America.

Additional to undertaking training, I am also involved with one-to-one coaching/mentoring, consulting, writing, assessing and examining for professional institutes' qualifications. This has included being Chief Examiner on the Graduate Diploma of the Chartered Institute of Purchasing and Supply and as an external university examiner for an MSc in Purchasing and Logistics.

Married to the lovely Christine and with two adult cute children, Jill and James; James is married to Mairead, who is also cute. We are additionally the proud grandparents of twin girls (the totally gorgeous, Megan and Molly).

I can be contacted at stuart@learnandchange.com or by visiting www.learnandchange.com. I do welcome any comments.

1.0. Understanding the Supply Chain

In this section we look at the following:

- The Supply Chain: an Introduction
- The Supply Chain and the Theory of Constraints
- Supply Chain History
- Supply Chain Growth
- The Value Chain and Competitive Advantage
- The benefits of a supply chain management approach
- Lead time
- Customer service
- Adding value
- Transactional or collaborative approaches
- Problems in integrating supply chains
- Type I and type II supply chains: a contrast

The Supply Chain: an introduction

The term Supply Chain is the process, which integrates, coordinates and controls the movement of goods, materials and information from a supplier through a series of customers to the final consumer. The essential point with a supply chain is that it links all the activities between suppliers and customers to the consumer in a timely manner. Supply chains therefore involve the activities of buying/sourcing, making, moving, and selling. The supply chain "takes care of business" following from the initial customer/consumer demand. Nothing happens with supply until there is an order; it is the order that drives the whole process. Indeed, some people logically argue that the term supply chain could be called the demand chain.

So the Supply Chain bridges the gap between the fundamental core business aspects of Supply & Demand, as shown below:

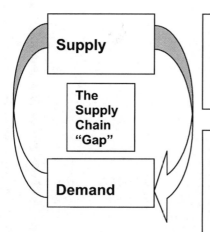

For example:
When is the product made?
Where is it made?
Which suppliers?
How much and how many are required?
How and when is it delivered?

For example:
When is the product required?
Where is it needed?
How many and when are needed?
What is the mix required?
How is it required?
What distribution network to use?

The philosophy of Supply Chain Management is to view all these processes as being related holistically so that they:
- Integrate, coordinate and control
- the movement of materials, inventory and information
- from suppliers through a company to meet all the customer(s) and the ultimate consumer requirements
- in a timely manner.

A diagrammatic view follows, where it will be seen that the flows of products and the flows of information are represented by ideas, order creation, and cash/orders:

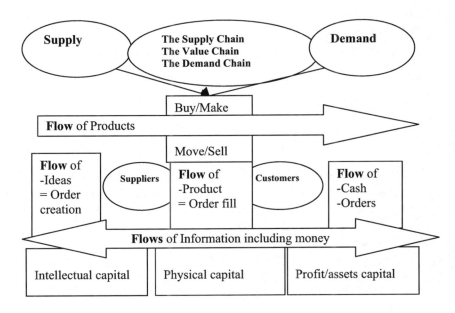

In the above diagram:
- The demand chain represents the creation of demand, for example, marketing and selling with product development.
- The supply chain represents fulfilment, for example, procurement and buying, production and making with distribution and moving.
- The value chain represents performance, for example, financial measures and capital.

The activities of Buying-Making-Moving and Selling take place in the operational functions of Purchasing, Production, Distribution and Marketing. If each of these functions were to work independently, then inventory stock levels will increase not only internally, but also across the supply chains that feed in and out from a company.

It is also important to realise that each company has not one supply chain, but many, as it deals with different suppliers and has different customers. For each individual finished product or line item, whilst some of the buying, making, moving and selling processes will be identical or very similar, the total supply chain for each product will be different and will involve often a complex network. This also goes, for example, far beyond the first supplier and includes the supplier's supplier, then that supplier's supplier and so on.

Many companies in their supply chain management do not work on the supply chain in this way and often stop with the first level supplier; they seem to forget that the supply chain is effectively a large network of supplier/customer players.

Additionally, different types of business and industry sectors will have different views of what the supply chain is about for them, for example:
- Retailers are driven by customer demand creation and the availability/fulfilment of a variety of products
- Oil companies are driven by production, so supporting production by the supply side is of more importance
- Car assemblers are more consumer demand driven, meaning closer integration of the supply and demand sides

Different business may be classified, as follows, that shows the influences of the operating environments. The key driver is highlighted:

	High Complexity	Low Complexity
High Uncertainty	Capital intensive industries: Aerospace Shipbuilding Construction **Fitness for purpose** (of product)	Fast moving consumer goods: Cosmetics Textiles Food and drink **Time** to market
Low Uncertainty	Consumer goods: Automotive White goods Electrical goods **Value for money**	Staple primary industries: Paper Glass Simple components **Price** (from production productivity)

Multiple and Globalised Supply Chains

As supply chains differ, then multiple supply chain management is perhaps a better description but it is a cumbersome one. At a simple level, consider the following globally reaching supply chain (part only), for Lee Cooper jeans:

Customers: Worldwide and buy from agents, wholesalers and retailers who have received finished products from a factory in Tunisia that gets supplies of:

- Denim cloth from Italy, who use dye from West Germany and cotton from Benin, West Africa and Pakistan
- Zips from West Germany, who uses wire for the teeth from Japan and polyester tape from France
- Thread from Northern Ireland, who use dye from Spain and fibre from Japan
- Rivets and Buttons from USA, who use zinc from Australia and copper from Namibia

- Pumice (used in stonewashing) from Turkey

With supply chain management therefore, there are many different supply chains to manage. These supply chain networks will contain companies from all the main following sectors; many of these will be globally located:

- Primary sector: Raw materials from farming/fishing (food, beverages, and forestry), quarrying/mining (minerals, coals, metals) or drilling (oil, gas, water)
- Secondary sector: Conversion of raw materials into products ; milling, smelting, extracting, refining into oils/chemicals/products and then maybe; machining, fabricating, moulding, assembly, mixing, processing, constructing into components, sub assembly's, building construction/structures and furniture's/electronic/food/paper/metal/chemicals and plastic products
- Service or tertiary sector: business, personal and entertainment services, which involve the channels of distribution from suppliers to customers, via direct, wholesale or retail channels. Services include packaging, physical distribution, hotels, catering, banking, insurance, finance, education, public sector, post, telecoms, retail, repairs etc.

Companies will therefore have many supply chains both internally and externally that interact through a series of simple to complex networks.
These networks can be domestic, international or global in reach. As Ronald Regan once famously said, "we now live in a global village."

Flows of Materials and Information and Money

In organising the material flows from any national, international or global locations, then the following will be required:

- Forecasting of the demand requirements
- Sourcing and buying from vendors/suppliers. At some stage, in this "supply cycle", there will be a manufacturer/producer involved. These may possibly be well down the supply chain when the supplier is an agent, a "trader" or a wholesaler or some other kind of "middle person".
- Transport
- Receiving, handling, warehousing and possibly, storing

The material flows are triggered by information, as information is needed for decision making. Information is also used to:

- Implement other activities
- Plan
- Organise
- Direct and coordinate
- Control

Information flows therefore link internal company activities and also link external suppliers and customers. Effective information, communication technology (ICT) will process orders, track and trace progress and provide timely and real time visibility.
The supply cycle information loop covers:

- forecasts
- buying
- purchase order and transactions
- stock information

The demand or customer cycle information loop covers:

- stock information
- replenishment and picking/order assembly
- transport and delivery
- invoicing
- payment

The integration of the supply and demand information loops gives an integrated system.
It will be seen also that **money flows** are also involved as information integrates materials and money flows. The design of the supply chain will determine the following monetary aspects:

- Asset investment, for example, this is minimised by outsourcing.
- Inventory holding and carrying costs, for example, from decisions on stock holding policy
- Debtors balances, for example, the customer order cycle times
- Creditor balance, for example, from holding lower stock levels
- Exchange rate variations from non domestic trade, for example by balancing the material flows

It is the planning, organising and controlling, of these "total/whole/holistic" material, information and money flows, which supply chain management, will provide competitive advantage. This is why Professor Martin Christopher noted the future is one of competing interdependent supply chains and not from individual companies operating independently. Individual companies therefore need to work together to manage the flows. These flows are determined by demand; therefore demand "pulls" the product, in turn meaning flexible response is need from "upstream", so as to satisfy the "downstream" information flows demand. Supplier bases may therefore have to be rationalised, as not all will be able to provide any new requirements for flexible, on time, in full deliveries; this is a requirement for demand driven supply chains.

Start at "home"

The starting point however, must be to firstly examine the internal supply chain. Too many companies start into Supply Chain Management (with much time and effort), by working "only" with the closest suppliers and customers. They should however first ensure that all their internal operations and activities are "integrated, coordinated and controlled." Companies may usefully ask their suppliers and customers, if their internal supply chain is working well; they may be surprised by the answer. Reorganising internally means ensuring that say production, procurement, logistics, marketing; or whatever are the functions involved, do not operate as shown below:

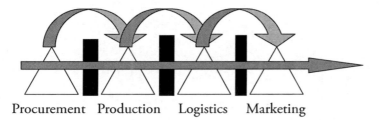

Procurement   Production   Logistics   Marketing

Here we see that effectively there are walls between each function, creating a barrier to the flows of goods and information. Instead of these flowing smoothly and horizontally across the functions, they are actually being "thrown over the wall", not only taking longer, but also increasing the chance of damage. We therefore need to ensure that all internal operations and activities are "integrated, coordinated and controlled" so that we have them working together and joined up, as shown below:

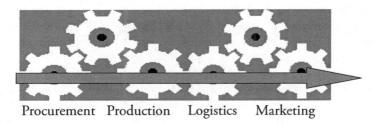

Procurement   Production   Logistics   Marketing

We will look later at how to get effective internal organisational structures.

Manage the inventory

In the supply chain, the flows of goods and information will need coordinating to minimise inventory levels. Levels of inventory that are too high can be viewed as the main "poorly" symptom of a supply chain and a root cause that needs "treatment". Additionally and as noted above, in supply chain management there are many different supply chains to manage and these supply chains will usually contain companies in many different sectors; all of these companies in the network can have "poorly" inventory.

As has been said, holding stock is an admission of defeat in supply chain management. Stock holding is anti-flow and can be analogous to water flowing. Water does not always flow evenly and at the same pace everywhere along a stream. Water sometimes gets trapped in deep pools, is blocked by rocks and other obstacles hidden below the surface. These rock and obstacles impede the smooth swift flows of the stream.

Here the stream represents the flow of goods and information in the supply chain. The pools of water are the inventory holdings and the rocks/obstacles; represent the waste in the process from poor quality, re-ordered goods, returned goods etc. If a steam is to flow fast and clear, then the rocks and obstacles have to be removed. To do this, the water (and inventory) level has to be lowered so that the rocks are exposed. Inventory can therefore be hiding more fundamental problems that are currently being hidden from view. As such inventory can be seen as the "root of all evil" in the supply chain.

Inventory is therefore the common component throughout the total Supply Chain; the format of inventory being raw material, sub assemblies/work in progress or finished goods (which are often held at multiple places in the supply chain). The format of inventory and where it is held is of common interest to all supply chain players and must therefore be jointly investigated and examined.

The Supply Chain and the Theory of Constraints

A useful overview of what fundamentally supply chain management involves is provided by the Theory of Constraints (TOC) of E. Goldratt and detailed in books such as "The Goal." TOC sees that any business is basically about:

*   Money
*   Sales
*   And the rates of movement involved in these two

TOC has therefore clear implications for supply chain management. We will briefly look at some of its important contributions. TOC sees that "Money and Sales" are connected as follows:

*   Throughput: The rate at which money is generated by sales (and by the time it taken "to move" through the system)
*   Inventory: The purchase of things that are held to maintain the throughout and the holding of finished goods. It is the money invested in things, intended to sell/awaiting sales
*   Costs: The money spent, turning inventory into sales

TOC notes that how these connections are viewed, has now changed, for example:

	Throughput	Inventory	Cost
Past View	Second	Third	First "The cost world"
View needed now	First "The throughput world"	Second	Third

This is an interesting perspective as it clearly reverses the view held by those companies who only major on cost control and marginalise all the other aspects.

The importance however, of "more than cost" perspectives is well supported by many recent approaches in supply chain management that do emphasise, for example, variable customer service comes from varied rates of throughput and movement. These are the critical aspects that are, refreshingly, included in the "throughput world" of TOC. Similarly, procurement approaches on total cost of ownership/whole life costs/total acquisition cost are all attempts to look wider than just superficial aspects such as the "cost price."

It can also be seen, that in the traditional input/output diagram of a business, we have the following:

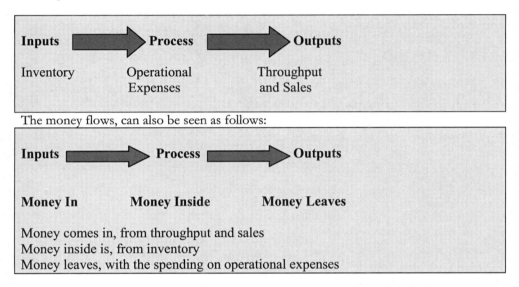

The money flows, can also be seen as follows:

Putting the above together indicates that the aim of supply chain management is to:

- Reduce inventory (and reduce the money tied up internally)
- Reduce operational expenses (and reduce the money leaving the company)
- Increase sales/throughout (and increase the money coming into the company)
- Do all the above, at the same time and in balance

This of course is not always going to be easy, especially when dealing with processes that are being independently managed and have opposing objectives and conflicts between the processes. A better "overall total process management" may be needed.

A process may be defined as "a sequence of dependent events, involving time, which has a valued result for the eventual end user." Processes also are selected portions of larger streams of activity that can be transformational (for example, in converting inputs to outputs) and can be transactional (for example, in exchanging outputs for new inputs).

The three key features of processes therefore are dependencies, variability's and interfaces. Looking at each of these in turn we can see:

Dependence:

- Is sequential and related ("knock on effects")
- Receives inputs and changes them to outputs
- What happens "here", causes events "there"
- "A" often needs to be finished, before "B" can start
- Any process, will be as efficient as its most inefficient part ("a chain is as strong as its weakest link")
- The most important factor is therefore, the most limiting one

Variability

- Displays statistical influences (e.g. a normal distribution curve), which is especially found with lead times
- Is when the "fixed, known, and expected" can become "variable, unknown and unexpected"
- Can cause changes from a state of "certainty" to "uncertainty"
- When each part of the process has variability, this causes knock on effects, to other processes, with sometimes, catastrophic results

Interfaces

- Are the potential friction points between processes
- Are often ignored, as our minds concentrate on "the inside of the box" and what happens there
- Real dependencies also exist in/at the interface

Therefore, features of processes also effectively describe supply chains. It also links with TOC where throughput is critical and is seen occurring at the rate of the last dependency. Throughput is consequently influenced by the fluctuating rates of the other dependencies and as the chain of dependencies increases (for example with long or variable/unreliable supply lead times), then there are going to be:

- Increases in inventory (as hold more to cover the variability)
- Increases in operating expenses (e.g. from the holding/carrying costs of inventory)
- Decreases in throughput (e.g. as the movement slows)

Supply Chain History

In the UK the history of the supply chain can be viewed as passing through three phases. However, with any such stereotyping there is much overlap, but at least an "ideal-typical" view is provided that enables key areas to be viewed more clearly (table 4 overleaf):

Attribute	Functional Supply Chains To the 1980s	Responsive Supply Chains The 1990s	Adaptive Supply Chains The Naughties
Integration focus	Over the wall	Transactional	Collaboration
	Reactive/Quick fixes	Responsive	Decision/ Proactive
	Monopoly suppliers	Competition in suppliers	Joined up networks of enterprises
Customer focus	Customer can wait	Customers wants it soon	Customer wants it now
	"You will get it when we can send it"	"You will have it when you want it"	"You will get it"
Organisation focus	Departmental and ring fencing.	Intra-enterprise. "Internal" involvement.	Extended enterprise involvement.
Product positioning	Make to stock	Assemble to order	Make to order
	Decentralised stock holding	Centralised stock holding	Minimal stock holding
	Store then deliver	Collect and cross dock	Whatever is needed
Management approach	Hierarchical	Command and control	Collaborative
Technology focus	Point solution	ERP	Web connected
Time focus for the business	Weeks to months	Days to weeks	Real time
Performance focus	Cost	Cost and service	Revenue and profit
Collaboration	Low	Medium	High levels
Response times	Static	Medium	Dynamic

Meanwhile on a more general basis, IBM has the following Supply Chain Maturity Model that also shows developments and differences in using the supply chain philosophy (table 5 opposite).

	Static SC	Functional excellence SC	Horizontal integrated SC	External collaboration SC	On demand SC
Processes and products	Ad hoc processes. "Over the wall". Production is focussed on standard products.	Formalised processes. Limited market research.	Formal processes. Internal integration. Cross functional teams.	Joint product designs with suppliers and customers. Coordinated product launches.	Formal integrated process with suppliers and customers
Customer Demand	Quarterly and manually produced plans. Frequent over and under stocks.	Some system generated planning. High inventory levels.	Forecast sharing with some suppliers. Internally integrated planning.	Customer "pull". Supplier partnerships. Daily planning.	Automatic adjustments to buying, making, and moving processes.
Buying	Unknown spend by commodity. No formal supplier relationships. All buying is done in house.	Master contracts with key suppliers. Central managed supply management.	Cross functional leveraged buying. SLA's with key suppliers.	Integrated supply network. Several procurement functions are outsourced. Central sourcing organisation.	Virtual outsourced network. Visibility of order's inventory, forecasts and shipments.
Customer fulfilment and logistics	Many logistics networks. No logistics outsourcing.	Some outsourcing of logistics. Different services to key customers. Some online customer ordering.	Enterprise integration. Common use of outsourcing logistics and contract manufacturing. Cross functional visibility. Differentiated services with customer segmentation.	Integrated distribution network with customers. Common outsourced partners. Visibility on total order to order cash cycle. Demand driven with managed replenishment.	Open network with rapid reconfiguration. Variable cost structures. All non cores is outsourced. End to end performance monitoring with alert exceptions.

Source: IBM "Follow the leaders"

Supply Chain Growth

Supply chains have grown like the UK road system. Roads developed over time from basic tracks between local supply and demand centres and they tended to be built in line with the environment, for example, taking an indirect route around hills and down valleys. This contrasts with the more recent motorway networks that cover more direct movements and, hopefully, a holistically designed network that also separates out fast and slow movers. The developments in roads and in supply chain management have therefore been similar:

- Simple to complex
- Indirect to direct
- Mixed to separated flows
- Slow to fast movement

As supply chains have grown and developed, there have been many words used to describe supply chain management. The following can be observed; again, the following stages do "blur" and are not mutually exclusive.

Main Concentration and Aim	Names used and Time Period	Flow type and the main parts involved
Sheds/trucks	Warehousing and Transport is "separated." 1950s	Physical flows "Move"
Physical networks and inventory reduction	Physical distribution management (PDM). 1960s	Physical flows "Move"
Centralised inventory	Material Management + PDM. 1970s	Physical Flows "Buy-make-move"
Eliminate inventory	Logistics management. 1980s	Physical + information "Buy-make-move-sell"
Continuous replenishment	Supply chain management. 1990s	Physical + Information "Buy-make-move-sell"
Zero lead time and total visibility	Demand pipeline management. 2000s	Physical+ Information "Buy-make-move-sell"

Whether the word demand pipeline management will become common, remains to be seen. However it does reflect the supply is "kick started" by demand and that without demand, there is no supply chain. Additionally, the pipeline analogy can be usefully applied, as one of the main aims for Supply Chain Management is for smooth flows of goods and information that are instantly available "on tap" from a pipe. This analogy however should not be taken to suggest that the supply chain represents is a linear and seamless fixed pipe with a stable, controllable, and self propelling flow, which is sealed from outside influences. Supply chains are rarely like this and for example, external influences can disrupt plans and expectations for the supply chain. Additionally as will be seen later, linear supply chain thinking can be very limiting and restrictive.

	"Steady as we go" approaches	"Lets go, get ready" approaches
Business	Individual business process decision-making.	Collaborative integrated fluid approaches.
	Fixed organisational structures.	Dynamic and changing flexible structures.
	Steady and slow economic growth.	Unpredictable growth.
	Long product life cycles.	"Fashion" and shorter product life cycles.
	Passive with at best, reactive management.	Proactive management
	Fixed costs.	Variable costs.
Technology	Standards IT systems.	Open integrated systems.
	Labour intensive.	Automated and self-managing.
	Users adapt to the technology.	Technology adapts to users

The Value Chain and Competitive Advantage

Some observers have the view of the supply chain representing a value chain that offers competitive advantage. The supply chain is therefore seen as the source of competitive advantage which simply means "doing it better" and/or "doing it cheaper" than competitors. In supply chain terms, this means the following:

Cost Leadership	Service Differentiation
Standard products produced cheaply	Customer designed products
Production push	Market pull
Flow and mass volume production, with high mechanisation	Job shop production with low mechanisation
Low inventory	Flexible and varied inventory
Focus on productivity	Focus on creativity
Stable planning	Flexible planning
Centralisation	Decentralisation
Standardisation	Bespoke and "one-offs"
Low level people	High level people

Michael Porter of Harvard Business School in his book "Gaining Competitive Advantage" introduced the value chain concept in 1985. From the diagram overleaf, you will see this has large implications for the supply chain:

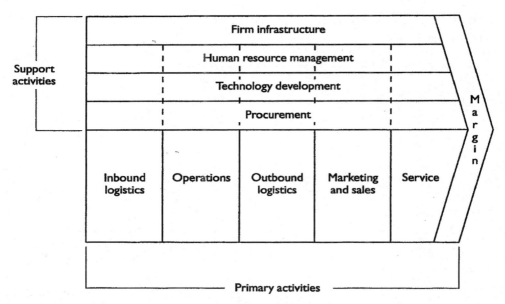

This divides into primary and support activities as follows:

Primary Activities

- Inbound logistics covering stores, warehousing, handling and stock control
- Operations covering production and packing and all activities that transfer inputs into outputs
- Outbound logistics include transport and warehouse networks to get products to customers
- Marketing and sales cover the methods by which customers know about and purchase products
- Service includes the support for all activities such as installation, returns.

Support Activities

- Procurement includes the buying and purchasing of products as well as all other resources
- Technology covers things information and communications technology (ICT) and research and development (R&D)
- Human Resource management covers all aspects concerned with personnel
- Infrastructure covers finance, legal and other general management activities

Porter then expanded this concept of a Value Chain into a Value System. This consists of a series of linked value chains. By this joining together of value chains into a value system, in effect we create a supply chain. Where the value actually is, according to Porter, is dependant on the way that a customer uses the product and not just totally on the costs incurred into buying, making and moving it. These costs include all the raw materials and activities that create the product, which then represents its value. But it is only when the product is purchased that the value can be measured and it is not until the product is at the final customer/consumer that the real value is to be found.

A difficulty here in reality, is that each individual organisation in the supply chain will attempt to define value themselves by looking at its own profitability. Each company will in turn carry on this definition to their suppliers and as the value definition, moves back up the chain, it will become distorted. Indeed, one important reason for companies to try to work together more closely with suppliers and customers is to have a constant view of value throughout the supply/value chain.

The benefits of a supply chain management approach

As has already been noted, competition in business can come not just from companies competing against each other, but increasingly comes from competing supply chains where, competitive advantage is to found by doing things better or by doing things cheaper.

Looking for these advantages extends from within a company, towards, the supply chains. This will mean looking to remove sub functional conflicts from all the interdependent processes, whether these processes are internal or external to a business. Accordingly, it is the supply chain that now provides the competitive advantage for a business.

This will in turn mean taking a total supply chain approach to examine and to total the costs of all the functions, matched to the service levels. If this is not done, and by continuing to minimise the costs for each sub function, then this could mean:

*   Buying in bulk from multiple sources (Purchasing is only being optimised); but for example, this will give high storage costs
*   Making few products with long production runs (here Production is only being optimised); which means limited ranges, poor availability etc.
*   Moving in bulk (Transport only being optimised); but gives infrequent delivery etc.
*   Selling what is produced (Marketing only being optimised); but it may not be needed

Supply chain structure and benefits

The way the supply chain is structured and managed is therefore critical and some reported benefits of adopting a supply chain approach follows. It will be significantly noted that different approaches give different results (table 9 overleaf):

	No Supply Chain: Functional Silos	Internal Integrated Supply Chain	Plus, External Integration to the first level only
Inventory days of supply Indexed	100	78	62
Inventory carrying cost % sales	3.2%	2.1%	1.5%
On time in Full deliveries	80%	91%	95%
Profit % Sales	8%	11%	14%

It will be seen that with a supply chain approach; inventory costs fall, with profit and the service fulfilment increasing; the "best of both worlds" for the company undertaking the approach. This however must start internally ("win the home games first").

Working together internally and organisational structure

We noted earlier that there is a need to ensure that all internal operations and activities are "integrated, coordinated and controlled" so that we have them working together and joined up, as shown below:

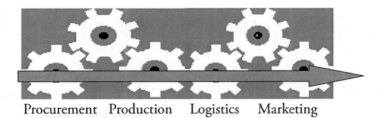

Procurement   Production   Logistics   Marketing

An organisation must therefore be appropriately structured towards for example, a cross functional model (CFM) so that it is able to effectively practice supply chain management. There will be a need to remember peoples career paths and guard against having a matrix structure with potential for unclear accountabilities and "in-fighting" over responsibilities, There is never an easy way to construct a CFM and it will need careful compromise on all of the following:

Organise around processes and not tasks
- Separate management from operational supervision. Management is generalised and at senior levels. Supervision is about the people actually doing the work

16

- Operations may remain hierarchical and functional, reporting into (several) process based managers
- Operational supervisors will need training in cross functional appreciation

Flatten the hierarchy
- Organise the hierarchy according to the level and type of work and responsibility; and not the number of people. For example, warehouse operatives and courier vehicle drivers at ratios to management of 10 plus to 1 and 30 plus to 1 respectively.

Keep a team focus
- This encourages self management.
- Ensure there are clear SMART objectives with the reward mechanism being the team performance
- Develop multiple competencies

More suppliers - customers contact
- Remember these are the next links in the process and are irrespective of whether they are internal and external suppliers/customers
- The customer is the only one who can give relevant feedback on how we do the job

From some most useful approach research undertaken by R. I. van Hoek and A. J. Mitchell (2006), we have a summary of some action items needed to ensure internal alignment in organisations:

Peers
- Support exchange programmes and job rotations across functions
- Invest and understand each other's problems and build relationships: capture the voice of other functions and be able to articulate plans in their language, not our jargon
- Develop appropriate KPIs across functions; ensure that KPIs are linked or at least coordinated and are not driving conflicting behaviour
- Joint problem solving teams to tackle common issues

Individuals
- Trace and learn from the cause of lost orders – delivery time, price, specification
- Encourage open communication
- Avoid pointing blame
- Visit & "see, smell, understand customers – get under their skin"
- Create regular dialogue between sales and supplying units

Bosses
- Join sales on key customer visits to ensure you are close enough to the customer in driving the supply chain agenda and focusing efforts and service and be credible with sales when discussing service
- Align goals between functions and link these to incentives
- Encourage the use of the same language; avoid functional jargon and promote the use of business language (profit, customers, service etc.)

- Support appropriate forecasting tools
- Ensure that operations/supply chain people are seen to take action on old issues and communicates the results to other functions (don't forget to tell others what has been done, there is no way that others know when you don't tell them)

Teams
- Collaborate on common issues not functional pet-projects
- Reach consensus on priorities; do not set a functional agenda but a company wide focus that will engage peers
- Work on improving accuracy of performance information and tell peers upfront when shipments are going to be late, do not surprise peers with bad events when they happen
- Awareness training in supply chain and sales
- Improve the initiative planning process to focus on essentials peers care most for mostly (service, execution, price etc.) and articulate initiatives in those terms

Internal alignment is critical for effective supply chain management. However it is often external people, like suppliers and customers, which are the first to realise when this alignment is not existent.

Working together externally

The additional benefits of supply chain management will only come when there is an examination of all costs/service levels together with all the external players with an aim to obtain reduced lead times and improved total costs/service for all the parties in the network. This means therefore, going beyond the first tier of suppliers and looking also at the supplier's supplier and so on. It represents more than data and process; it includes mutual interest, open relationships and sharing. The optimum and the "ideal" cost/service balance will only ever be found by working and collaborating with all players in the supply chain. This is an important topic and we shall come back to it later.

A key area here is to balance the service aspects with the costs. A significant part of business cost will be found in the Supply Chain and managing all of the flows of goods and information across the supply chain networks is therefore essential in bringing about the required cost/service balance. A big promise and often never an easy approach but one that can result in the perfect ideals of:

- Increased/improved service, reaction times, product availability etc.
- Reduced/improved total cost, total stock levels, time to market etc.

Doing things differently can improve performance and where costs rise and market prices are unable to be increased, then a new style of supply chain management can be beneficial, as shown in the following case study:

Case Study: Construction and Wolesley Supply Chain

The UK Construction Industry

Construction is one of the UK's largest industries, contributing 10% to the UK's GDP, its output is three times that of agriculture and larger than any single manufacturing industry It also has the largest workforce, employing more than two million people. However, despite the significant advances in design, product and process innovation by a vanguard of enlightened companies, the majority of the UK construction industry, particularly at grass roots level, retains many inefficient and outdated practices, which have long since disappeared other industry sectors. One of the biggest challenges facing the sector, at a time when skilled labour is increasingly rare and expensive, is the need to ensure that when labour is available it is used productively to increase project efficiency. That means getting materials to the right place at the right time.

The report of the "Rethinking Construction" Task Force, published in July 1998, highlighted logistics and supply chain management as one of many areas where the UK construction industry could improve, particularly by taking note of and learning from, the ways in which other industry sectors operate. The report cited 'lean' processes, as used in the car industry as a vital means of obtaining sustained improvements in performance a bringing the construction sector up to standards being achieved in many other of industry. Six years on, there is still much work to inefficiency and waste remains barriers to improved performance for many in the construction supply chain.

Wolseley

Wolseley UK, one of the largest distribution companies of construction, heating and plumbing materials, is one of the enlightened companies within construction which has seen that sophisticated logistics practices and robust supply chain management are essential to achieving sustainable improvement. Garry Flanagan is director of logistics at Wolseley UK. He sees the company's role as being the 'lynchpin' in the supply chain, which brings materials from the manufacturers to the sites where they are needed. Flanagan says: "As a sophisticated merchant at the hub of the supply chain, Wolseley UK can eliminate inefficiency and waste in a number of ways. With a national network of distribution centres and branches, we are ideally placed to distribute materials efficiently and provide valuable, local storage capacity. This eliminates the problem of leaving materials on-site, vulnerable to damage and shrinkage and taking up valuable site space.

"The use of a sophisticated logistics system can ensure that materials are delivered on site at exactly the right time. In the most successful cases, a carefully managed merchant-contractor relationship can make it possible to deliver to 30-minute windows into brown field construction sites in urban areas. The close relationship merchants have with contractors and sub-contractors and their logistics and supply chain systems mean that they can provide the right supply solution for each client. We are able to provide our customers with an integrated solution and offer a hassle free one-stop-shop for our customers' procurement teams."

Efficiency gains

Wolseley UK's highly sophisticated hub and spoke network of distribution centres across the UK plays a crucial role, enabling fast delivery of most of its vast range of products as well as rapid replenishment of stocks across its 1,500-plus branches The distribution centre (DC) at Melmerby, North Yorkshire, is the company's newest facility.

With a comprehensive product range and a highly automated operation, the Melmerby DC is an extremely efficient operation, which is setting standards for the rest of the UK. The automation provided by VanDerLande Industries is controlled by a computerised system linked to the warehouse management system which, in turn, is linked to the host stock file, and ordering and replenishment system. Wolseley UK has also used its extensive distribution network to take cost out of the extended supply chain (the combined Supplier-Wolseley UK supply chain). This is done by integrating suppliers' and Wolseley UK's supply lines to share the benefit of the resulting efficiency gains. Flanagan continues: "Our national network of distribution centre and branches enables us to provide an unrivalled delivery promise and nationwide access to our products and services. We provide our customers with a variety of added-value services, and ensure a tailored approach to their needs including direct delivery from our distribution centres and off-site prefabrication. The Wolseley UK trade park initiatives and express high street branches also offer customers even greater accessibility to our products and a higher level of convenience."

The company is streamlining operations and maximising the efficiencies across all seven of its operating brands — Plumb Center, Build Center Hire Center, Climate Center, Parts Center Pipe Center and Drain Center.

Partnership and reduced costs

Wolseley UK and Taylor Woodrow are piloting a partnership scheme on a housing development in Bromsgrove. It is the first time a partnership of this kind has been undertaken with a house builder. The company has a mini- branch on site, and through close liaison with the site manager and links to both Wolseley UK and Taylor Woodrow's IT systems on-site, it manages all of the ordering and delivery of materials on Taylor Woodrow's behalf.

The only materials brought on site are those that are needed. Wolseley's bulk distribution sites at Dudley and Northampton package the materials for each specific unit and they are either delivered direct to the plot or held in an on-site compound ready for delivery the following day. Smaller items are assembled into plot lots on site. The main challenge that Wolseley and Taylor Woodrow have faced is the resistance to change, which is ingrained in the culture of the industry. This resistance means it can take a lot of effort and a long time to make progress, reach agreement and establish terms and conditions. However, having seen the partnership in action this resistance is melting away, but it has taken absolute proof of the benefits to convince people that the old method of procurement was not necessarily the best. With materials taken care of, the site manager is free to concentrate on the build programme. Having more time to spend working with sub-contractors means problems can be identified and overcome quickly which leads to improved quality and less snagging at the end of the build phase, which reduces costs and avoids tying up skilled labour for longer than is absolutely necessary. Before the pilot, the site manager spent 60% of his time chasing materials and managing deliveries. This has been reduced by 50% and when the pilot moves to phase two, where all subcontractors also buy through Wolseley UK this will reduce further.

The project is currently ahead of schedule and in the interests of continuous improvement, Wolseley and Taylor Woodrow are working to establish and measure the financial savings, time savings and the increase in productivity that have resulted from this collaboration.

More changes needed

Wolseley UK is making great strides in improving efficiency and in developing supply chain solutions to meet customers' needs. In the industry at large, however a significant step change is still required to bring logistics and supply chain management up to the standards of many other commercial and industrial sectors. Flanagan comments: "The only way that the industry can make any real progress is by developing close partnerships between suppliers and customers and for supply chain integration to become part of the culture of construction. At Wolseley we are aiming to create more awareness of the issues of supply chain management within construction and are constantly reviewing our own supply chain. He continues: "Our team of supply chain professionals will focus on taking our supply chain to the next stage of development across warehousing, transport, demand and supply planning. We also have a supply chain development team, which will design and implement the strategy for Wolseley UK over the coming years. We are also focused on sharing best practice across the Wolseley group and beyond through a supply chain committee and we aim to achieve a results-based culture through key performance indicators and rewarding individuals and teams on the basis of their performance."

Through working with its supply base and customers, Wolseley UK will continue to take advantage of integration and collaboration opportunities to drive down cost and offer unrivalled service. "Collaboration and supply chain integration is the key to the successful future of construction logistics. Partnership with our suppliers enables us to share demand data to improve product availability and successfully bring new products to market. Partnership with our customers allows us to better understand their needs and provide a tailored end-to-end solution to their needs."

Extracts from source: Logistics Manager March 2005

Lead Time

Lead time is perhaps the critical component in supply chain management. However it is usually viewed incrementally and sub-optimally. Just as time is cash, and cash flow is important to a business, then also important are the associated flows of goods and information that have generated the cash flow in the first place. The cash to cash cycle time (C2C) is at the root of cash flow and reducing the time from buying to the receipt of payment for sales is therefore critical.

What follows is a basic view of lead time covering all the elements involved; first, by looking at the eight types of lead time; then followed by an analysis of the component parts of these eight types:

Eight types of Lead Time

Lead Time	Action	By
Pre order Planning	User	Customer
Procurement	Order placing	Customer to supplier
Supplier	Order despatching	supplier
Production	Making to order	supplier
Warehouse	Supplying from stock	supplier
Transit	Transporting	supplier
Receivers	Receiving	customer
Payment	Paying	Customer to supplier

Component parts of Lead times

Lead time	Lead Time Stage	Steps, by date
Pre Order Planning	User Need	Analysing status to determining need to order
	User Requisition	Need to order to date of order requisition
Procurement	Order preparation	Order requisition to order release date
	Order confirmation	Order release to date of confirmation
Supplier * see also the production and warehouse lead times	All the stages here are in the production and warehouse lead times	Confirmation to order despatched date
Production (e.g. made to order)	Order processing	Date of order receipt to date order accepted/confirmed
	Preparation	Order accepted to date manufacture starts

	Manufacture (Queue time, set up, machine /operator time/inspect/put away times)	Start of manufacture to date it finishes
	Pack/Load (to the Warehouse or to Transit LT)	Finished manufacture to date order despatched
Warehouse (e.g. available ex stock	In stock	Date goods arrived to date of order receipt
	Order Processing	Order receipt to date order is accepted or confirmed
	Picking	Date order accepted to date order is available/ picked
	Pack/Load (to Warehouse or to Transit LT)	Order available to date order despatched
Transit		Date despatched to date order received
Receiving		Date order received to date available for issue/use
Payment	Credit	Date invoice received or of other "trigger," to date payment received
	Payment processing	Date payment received to date cash available for use

Supply lead time

The supply lead time (SLT) should not be confused with the above mentioned supplier lead time. The supply lead time is actually the total of all the above lead times, excluding the payment lead times. Supply lead-time is the total time from the "start" of determining the "need", to the "end" of the product being available for use. This is shown below.

Supply and Supplier Lead Times

- Time decide need
- Time place order
- Time order received
- Time product despatched ⎤
- Time product received ⎬ Supplier LT
- Time available for issue ⎦
- Time payment available to supplier

⎫ Supply LT

Supply lead time therefore involves many processes such as:
- internal processes of the pre-order planning lead time from analysing the order status/ determining when to order, requisitions and authority "signing off" up to, the placing of an order
- the external supplier lead time from order receipt, to the delivering of the goods
- the internal process of the receiving lead time (date order received to checking and placing into store and notifying the system and users that the product is available for issue)

The supply lead time involves many different parties internally in a business and also externally, including both the supplier and the customer.

Lead time examination

Lead times must be examined using real examples, whilst ensuring that all appropriate stages and steps are included. There may also be additional lead times for some players, for example, the customs clearance lead-time with imports.

An example below, using chocolate confectionery shows some abbreviated results found on lead times:

- Supply lead time (Cocoa): 180 days on average (once per year crop) with a company in stock lead time of 70 days (traders also hold some external stocks)
- Supply lead time (Ingredients): for example, with nuts 80 days on average (range 10-120 days) and the in stock of 80 days maximum
- Supply lead time (Sugar) 1-2 days with in stock lead time of 2 days
- Supply lead time (Packaging): 1-3 days with in stock lead time of 3 days maximum
- Production lead time: 1-2 days but due to product line batch scheduling this can mean waiting for 30 days before the next production run
- Warehouse & transit lead times (Distribution): 1-5 days with in stock lead time of 30 days minimum to cover for the production lead time

After each lead time stage has been quantified, analysis will show if there is a way to do things better. It can be expected that many reductions in lead times will come from information flows and not from the goods flows.

Lead time variability

A crucial aspect when examining lead time is variability as when lead times are realistically looked at, then a range of times will be found; for example from 2 to 8 days. This range represents the variability of lead time and average calculations are of little practical assistance and can be dangerous if used for planning and decision making. It is this variability that so often represents the uncertainty found in the Supply Chain and which is traditionally dealt with by holding safety stocks to cover against the uncertainty. The variability must however be examined by all those involved, before finally working together to agree that lead times becomes a fixed item. Then the variability and the uncertainty are removed by having fixed known reliable lead times; the length of the lead time being of secondary importance.

The problem of lead variability can be illustrated as follows:

If: lead time (LT) is halved from 12 to 6 weeks and lead time variability (LTV) stays the same at ± 4 weeks, then:

Current LT	**New LT**
LTV LT LTV	LTV LT LTV
-4 12 + 4	-4 6 +4

Total LT	
8 to 16 weeks	2 to 10 weeks
(Index 100 to 200)	(Index 100 to 500)

So, if LTV stays the same, then there is higher disruption/costs and reduced speed (index of 1 to 2 from 1 to 5)

Reducing lead time variability

The following are some ways to consider in reducing lead time variability:

Demand LTV

- Predictable known orders/size/make up
- Predictable order times
- Data accuracy on what customers want/when/price
- Is it "end" demand or is it "institutionalised" through inefficient "not talking" supply chain players (internal and or external)

Supply LTV

- Predictable known LT
- Get correct quantity first time
- Get correct quality first time
- Data accuracy on what is supplied/price.

The importance of lead time in inventory can be seen in the expression, "uncertainty is the mother of inventory." The length of lead time is of secondary importance to the variability and uncertainties in the lead time. It is the variability that causes disruptions and results in stock outs, which in future are then covered by holding more stock, that then results in stock overages.

Time is cash, cash flow is critical and so are the goods and information flows; fixed reliable lead times are therefore more important than the length of the lead time.

Meanwhile, the following case study illustrates the importance of lead times to one major organisation:

Case Study: Lead Times Crunch at B&Q

Steve Willett, director of supply chain at B&Q, came to the firm last July from the US, where he worked for aerospace and engineering firm Allied Signal There, he was on the other side of the fence feeling the pressure that Wal-Mart puts on its suppliers. But he has come away with a profound admiration for the quality of supply chain management in the US and a burning ambition to mimic it in the UK. "We want to be a world-class supply chain that is talked about as a leader in the field," he says.

"Effective delivery performance by the supplier has to become a minimum requirement for doing business with B&Q. The norm of delivery is far better in the US than in the UK, but the supermarkets here have effectively driven up the performance of their suppliers and we are going to do the same for the DIY industry."

B&Q's wider strategy of slashing the retail prices of goods through savings has led to growth of between 25 per cent and 30 per cent a year for the past few years. However, it has also meant that savings are being constantly sought from the supply chain. Since September, Willett has put different supply chain projects in place, with Easter at the front of his mind.

"The Easter trading pattern is very significant because it is so concentrated and there is no time to recover," he says. On some seasonal lines, such as garden furniture, there is a 15-month lead-time, but on others, such as peat, the constraint is how many lorries the company can get on the ferries from Ireland.

At Easter, the line between store and warehouse often becomes a little blurred, with 40-foot containers sometimes sitting in the car parks to maximise the selling space inside the stores.

Project work

The supply chain projects, which have examined almost every aspect of the firm's supply process, have looked at:

- How handling can be minimised, so that stock can be taken from the delivery lorries to be stored on pallets in the 300 stores;

- Ensuring that space is given to the best-selling lines, so that they maintain a constant presence on the shelves;

- e-replenishment mechanisms;

- Ensuring that the five regional consolidation centres that handle stock from abroad are incorporated into the delivery from the four distribution centres;

- Ensuring that new procedures are put into place, with 30 implementation managers working in the stores.

Supplier development

Willett says this last one is not as sinister as it sounds: "We are not expecting overnight revolutions and saying to suppliers, 'perform or else'. It's a matter of working with them to set targets and help them to get there. Supply chain management is one of the company's biggest internal costs and, if we are to deliver savings to the customer, we have to become more efficient. There will be suppliers that will be too slow and unable to get there as we ratchet the bar down, and I have no doubt we will lose some along the way. But, with that said, we want to achieve a fairly stable supplier base and work with suppliers in partnerships."

Mark-Paul Homberger, B&Q's vendor performance manager, predicts that some household names will be de-listed from the firm's supplier base. B&Q has instituted a system of green, amber and red status for suppliers, where green signifies a fine relationship, amber that there will be no new business and red that they should sort themselves out or face being de-listed. "We have to ensure availability to the customer and if suppliers can't get their act together on lead times, we are absolutely serious that we will source elsewhere," explains Homberger. B&Q is going the same way as supermarket giants Tesco and Sainsbury's (owner of rival DIY chain Homebase), he suggests. "Our vendor-buying agreements will include agreed service levels and, crucially, lead times," he says. "When things fall apart at the seams, we need to know what the action plan is to recover. Often with domestic suppliers, poor performance can be attributed to the fact that they won't invest the capital, but we want to emphasise that it is really in the supplier's interest to give us a better deal."

Source: Supply Management 20 April 2000

Customer Service

This is commonly measured by the following on time, in full (OTIF) measurements:

- Cycle Lead Time (On time delivery or OT): e.g. Daily delivery service, order day 1 for day 2 delivery
- Stock Availability (In full delivery or IF): e.g. 95% orders met from stock
- Consistency/Reliability: e.g. 95% orders are delivered within 3 days

Actual achievement in companies varies; the following may be helpful for comparison purposes: (see table overleaf)

Key performance indicators – average figures from UK manufacturers
(Source: Best Factory Awards 2001)

Industry sector	On time delivery reliability	In full ex stock availability	Stock-turns per annum
Process	91.0%	97.5%	14
Engineering	92.0%	96.0%	13
Electrical	96.0%	98.2%	9
Consumer household	98.1%	99.0%	21

(These stock turns figures can be misleading. These are calculated from financial annual accounts by dividing the sales turnover, by the value of the stock assets on hand, to give an average yearly figure of stock asset value turn. This would not be the same as the physical stock turns.)

Customer importance
It is only the order from the customer that triggers all the activity in the supply chain. Without a customer order, then no supply chain activity is required. The customer is only interested in buying delivered products.

Customer service levels are a variable and each customer service variable has a cost associated with it. The relationship between cost and service is rarely linear, but more of an exponential curve. So for example, a 10 per cent increase in service may mean, a cost increase of 15 or, over 50 per cent. Other examples from transport are that we pay more for first class mail than for second class mail; we pay more for a service offering an overnight parcel delivery than for a three day or a deferred delivery.

Customer Value
Customers will place a value on many aspects of the total service offering. Value is placed by customers primarily against delivery/availability but also against quality, the cycle lead-time and the cost and the service levels. As perception is reality, different customers can see these as being inter-related or may view them independently. It is therefore important for a business to understand the specific reality as seen by the customer.
The following are the aspects of criteria that customer's value:

Quality is "performing right first time every time" and involves:
- Meeting requirements
- Fitness for purpose
- Minimum variance
- Elimination of waste
- Continuous improvement culture

Service, is about "continually meeting customer needs as the market changes", and involves:
- Support available
- Product availability
- Flexibility

- Reliability
- Consistency

Cost is about knowing what the costs really are and then looking at how to reduce them. This involves the:
- Design of product
- Manufacturing process
- Distribution process
- Administration process
- Stock levels

Cycle lead-time is about knowing what the lead times really are and then looking for ways to reduce them. This involves considering:
- Time to market
- Time from order placement to time available for issue
- Response to market forces

A business therefore, ideally will try to improve the quality and the service, whilst, reducing the cost and lead times. All of the aspects are inter-related and connected and for example, it matters not to the majority of customers where the goods come from or whether the goods are transported by road, rail, sea, air etc. After all, customers are interested in buying available or delivered goods.

The customer is the reason for the business - so - continually working to serve the customer better is critical. But who is the customer? The traditional view is perhaps the one that pays the invoices, but by seeing the next person/process/operation in the chain as the customer, then, this way of thinking means there may well be hundreds of supplier/customer relationships in a single supply chain. If all these "single" relationships were being viewed as supplier/customer ones, then the "whole" would be very different.

The Customer is the business; it is their demand that drives the whole supply chain; finding out what Customers value and then delivering it, is critical. The view of one major company, on customer service in the supply chain, is meanwhile illustrated below:

Case study: Wal-Mart: The Supply Chain and Customer Service

(Wal-Mart is the US Company that owns the UK Company, Asda)

Sam Walton and the Wal-Mart retail chain revolutionised the role of Logistics. Walton explains the Wal-Mart philosophy (Walton 1992): "Here's the point. The bigger Wal-Mart gets, the more essential it is that we think small...If we ever forget that looking a customer in the eye, greeting him or her, and asking politely if we can be of help is just as important in every Wal-Mart store today as it was in [first little store], then we just ought to go into a different business because we'll never survive in this one."

Wal Mart supply chain supports that vision by "thinking small" and observes the following points:

- **Serve one store at a time.**

The objective of the supply chain—serving customers—is achieved store by store, department by department, customer by customer.

- **Communicate, communicate, and communicate.**

Keep a constant flow of communication through meetings, phone calls, information system reports, pep talks, and seminars.

- **Keep your ear to the ground.**

Managers need to get out of their offices and into their facilities for a real "hands-on, get-down-in-the-store" perspective.

- **Push responsibility—and authority—down.**

Allow operations-level staff to be "managers of their own businesses," and to identify and implement improvements.

- **Force ideas to bubble up.**

Encourage managers to propose ideas for new ways to work.

- **Stay lean, fight bureaucracy.**

As organisations grow, duplication can build up. "If you're not serving the customer, or serving the folks who do, we don't need you."

Adding Value

This has become common language in business, but is often confused in its use and meaning. There seem to be two different views:

1) Value is found when something; satisfies a need, conformed to expectations and/or, gives "pride of ownership", i.e. it is "valued" over something that is not.

Here then the perception of value will differ. Maybe value is, simply, what the customer says it is; as customers will have different perceptions of "worth" and "price." For example, different customers have different perceptions of quality/lead time and the cost/service balance. Maybe therefore, value can be seen at the balance/pivot point between worth and price, quality and lead time and cost and service?

2) Value is the opposite to cost and in most processes, more time is actually spent on adding cost & not on adding value, for example:

- **In warehousing:**
  30 days in Storage (cost adding) yet only 1 day to Pick/Pack/Load/Transit to the customer (value adding)

- **In manufacturing:**   85% of time= cost adding with queuing/setting up/ inspecting/storing and handling.

    15% of time = value adding with processing/QA.

A business will not find it worthwhile to invest and automate wasteful non-value added activities. Waste is the symptom rather than the root cause of the problem. (The seven wastes are covered fully later in this book and are: overproduction, waiting, transporting, inappropriate processing, unnecessary inventory, unnecessary/excess motion and defects). So the aim must be to investigate the cause and then remove the wasteful non-value adders: those processes that take time and resources without adding any value, such as those costs below:

- Raw materials stocks
- Work in progress stocks
- Finished goods stocks
- Stock write offs/obsolescence
- Storage
- Waiting and Queuing time
- Inefficient processes
- Support activities

Attention should therefore be given to those activities that do add "real" value, for example:

- Make it faster, through Form changes (e.g. redesign a product)
- Move it faster, through Times changes (e.g. shorten the transit time)
- Get paid faster, through Place changes (e.g. sell Ex-Works)
- Serving the customer better

Some other examples of Adding Value in Supply Chains are:

From	To
Forecasting	Make to order
Inventory push and stock holding	Inventory pull from order placing
Storing	Sorting
Handling	Postponement
Manual ordering	Automated ordering

A supply chain view of added value would also recognise that it is only the movement to the customer that is adding (the ultimate) value. Stopping or delaying the flow, adds costs; as shown overleaf.

Cost and Value adders in the Supply Chain

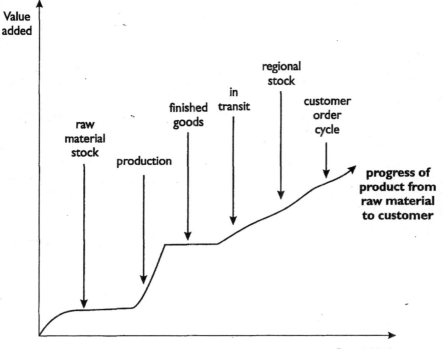

Clearly, this diagram shows that goods being stored are incurring cost and are not adding value. Whilst this will generally be the case, if those goods being stored were appreciating in value, then this would not apply. This would however only apply for a very limited range of products, such as with bullion (in non-inflation times) and with works of art.

The diagram emphasises that movement to the customer as quickly as possible whilst accounting for the associated cost levels, is what really counts in adding value. It is only the movement to the customer that adds the ultimate value; smooth continuous flow movements are therefore preferable.

The challenges to be faced here involve basically will involves doing things faster, for example, making products quicker, moving them into the marketplace faster and getting paid faster. Supplier rationalisation on the basis of product quality and reliability in lead time and delivery performance will be required. Distribution networks may also have to be rationalised to ensure product actually flows and is not being held and delayed.
In turn this means more challenges such as:

- Reducing inventory
- Responsive order processing
- Short and reliable last times from all involved in all processes

- Product received that is the "right quantity, right quality, at the right time and the right cost."
- Appropriate ICT
- Close working relationships and understanding of all the supply chain "players"

Changes in marketplaces now mean "customer specific" or customised products are required, leading to buying in smaller quantities required more flexible suppliers. This in turn will often mean that time is compressed, for example, from a past requirement of a weekly delivery of 26 pallets every Friday that has now changed to, 10 pallets at 1500 hours on Monday, 6 at 1000 Tuesday, 4 at 1300 Wednesday and 6 on Saturday at 0800 hours; with the subsequent weeks requirements being different.

This focuses in a specific supply chain on all of the current material and information lead times, the storage/static times and the payment/credit times; as well as the associated customer service requirements of availability, delivery schedules/frequencies and the requirement to provide continuous reliability over a long time period.

It is perhaps not surprising therefore that the trends and visible changes have been as follows:

- Product flows are synchronised with demand
- Reliable lead times, to give less uncertainty and reduce stock levels
- ICT improvements and developments
- Integration, internally and externally

Transactional or collaborative approaches

The differences in managing supply chains on a transactional/responsive basis or on a collaborative/adaptive supply chains makes an interesting comparison. Another "ideal-typical" comparison follows:

Transactional	Collaboration
Price/Risk	
Price orientation.	Total cost of ownership.
Price dominates.	Shared destiny dominates.
One way.	Two way exchanges.
Customer demands sensitive data.	Exchanges of sensitive data.
Customer keeps all cost savings.	Mutual efforts to reduce costs, times and waste.
All risk with supplier, the buyer risks little.	Shared risk and benefits.
"What is in it for me?"	"What is in it for us?"
Short term.	Long term

Continues overleaf...

Negotiations Strong use of ploys in negotiations. Power based. Win/lose. "One off" deals. "One night stand." Walk in and out of, change is easy. Easy to set up. Adversarial and maybe inefficient for one party. "Partnershaft."	Mutual gains "rule" discussions. Equality based. Win/win. "For ever" together. "Marriage." Difficult to break, change is difficult. Difficult to set up. Challenging to implement and continue with. Partnership.
Inter personal relationships No personal relationships. Separated/arms length. Low contact/closed. Predatory power based. Hierarchical /superior subordinate. Blame culture. Alienated employees.	Strong personal relationships. Close/alliance. Shared vision/open. Proactive and more people based. Equality. Problem solving "gain" culture. Motivated employees.
Trust Trust is based on what the contract says= contractual trust. Little ongoing trust. Power based "spin."	Trust is based on goodwill, commitment and cooperation. Continual trust plus risk/benefits sharing. Pragmatic "tough" trust.

The change from transactional methods to collaborative approaches goes far beyond the technical issues, of say ICT connectivity, and fully embraces the soft skills. If all the supply chain parties would work together then a lot more would get done more efficiently and more effectively. The evidence for this from relationship principles seems overwhelming yet many do not subscribe to any mutually sharing collaborative supply chain management approach.

Meanwhil,e the following paper gives some clues for arranging successful alliances:

Case Study: Strategic Alliances

Some of the common lessons learned from past experiences in putting together a variety of strategic alliances include the following:
- Give each other the benefit of the doubt
- Commitment and communication
- Keep bringing new ideas to the table
- People like to do business with friends (leverage relationships)
- Good for the buyer = good for seller
- Quick wins will ensure success of relationship
- Celebrate the successes
- Focus, execute and measure
- Time is of the essence
- Communicate the wins
- Measure what we're doing, set goals
- Keep in mind "Why" is this will be valuable to the customer (internal and external)
- Know the processes
- Create an environment for partnership
- Why 1 + 1 = 3? Why together? Why better?

Summary
The rewards to those buyer/seller organizations that maintain the commitment to the strategic alliance relationship can be significant and result in long term benefits. However, to achieve these benefits will require a commitment of time and resources, which typically exceeds that required for a traditional contractual relationship

Source: "Strategic Alliances: How to Make 1+1=3" by Michael Patton at ISM 91st Conference May 2006

Supply chain management collaboration between companies will not succeed without appropriate recognition that soft skill development is required; after all any relationship depends on trust and without trust, there is no relationship. Again very simple to say, yet many do not realise this and if they do, they do not practice it. An important topic we shall return to later.

Problems in integrating supply chains

As will have been seen already, the "theory" of effective and efficient supply chain management is relatively clear; it is the application and the management practices that are difficult. Supply Chain management is classic common sense; but then, whilst it may be sense, it is not very common.

Some of the reasons for this and the problems found in supply chain management are due to the following factors:

- Inaccurate forecasting of demand
- Volatile markets and demand patterns
- Unwillingness to share information
- Power "forcing" by large dominant customers/buyers
- Resistant "monopoly" suppliers
- Poor ICT
- Management styles and approaches
- Poor and unreliable delivery performance
- No control of supply or supplier lead time
- Global/long distance suppliers and or markets
- Resistance to change
- Lack of knowledge/resources
- Misunderstanding of how independently managed processes interact

To further these problems and difficulties, the following case study reflects wide ranging views of what is needed to re-structure UK manufacturing. The links to supply chain management principles are very clear.

Case Study: Restructuring UK Manufacturing Supply Chains

1) Restructure capital:
Emphasise has been on short-term growth which is "fashionable" to the city. However, long term investment is needed

2) Examine and invest in processes:
Examine waste in capital, process standardisation, product portfolio rationalisation, and work across the supply chain by:
- getting the internal supply chain correct: styles, culture, trust, communication
- developing a clear way forward: tangible deliverables, aligned accountabilities, adequate resources
- transparency: forecast and performance information with consistent actions
- driving time performance: lengths of time for each process,: total time, lead time excesses
- adding value with the process, not cost
- developing reliability for what is out of tolerance

3) Segment the portfolio:
- view each product as a separate supply chain with varied demands, product characteristics, operational capability, distribution channels, supplier profiles, and market dynamics
- install effective KPIs: to give visibility and to drive action
- install internal/customer/supplier relationships at each interface

4) Invest in product leadership:
Labour intensive, low value products are not the way forward, understand costs and trim lower margin products. Value add products are needed

5) Develops skills base:
Relying on others to train is not acceptable; this has been the problem from the last 20 years

6) Know the market:
Market research is needed.

7) Consolidate:
Critical mass is needed, as in automotive and electronics.

Source: Based on a report in SHD December 2002

Some manufacturing organisations have however, purposely chosen to manage their supply chains collaboratively and more proactively, as the following case study indicates.

Case Study: Collaboration and Proctor & Gamble

US owned group Procter & Gamble (P&G) manufactures and markets nearly 300 brands of consumer products including household names Lenor, Ariel, Pampers, Sunny Delight and Pringles. With a workforce of nearly 100,000 worldwide, the group operates in nearly 80 countries worldwide.

However its supply chain was inefficient. As a result the company has been transforming its UK supply chain into an efficient and collaborative operation. This process has involved implementing a range of innovative schemes to help optimise and consolidate the supply chain and the group's "first time fill rate" for customers now stands at 90%.

The transformation has proved so successful that the trailblazing ideas are now being introduced elsewhere within P&G's European supply chain.

The challenge of revolutionising the group's UK supply chain has been the responsibility of Chris Poole P&G's logistics director for the UK and Ireland and co-chair of consumer industry body ECR UK. The group's new philosophy, explains Poole, is all about "Winning at the first moment of truth. It is important that we make sure product is there at the store, looks good on the shelf, and has been delivered in the most cost-efficient way so that those cost savings can be ultimately incorporated into a lower cost. That's not new. It's just about great service and low costs, and trying to get that balance".

For P&G there are two moments of truth:

- "On the shelf' — if consumers get to the shelf and the product is not there, they cannot buy it. The moment of truth here is whether the consumer will remain faithful to P&G's product or choose a rival's.

- The second moment of truth is when the consumer, having bought the product, gets it home. Will the product do what it says it will?

The transformation of P&G's UK supply chain began after three areas were identified that had to be dealt with in order to deliver a great on-shelf service. Poole explains: "The first is that we have to deliver a great basic service, we have to be good at the fundamentals. We don't have the licence to do anything else with customers unless we are fantastic at that. Secondly, we have to and want to collaborate very closely with customers. We can't do it by ourselves. And thirdly, we must work now on the future. We have to be innovative."

Poole continues: "That's different to what it was maybe five to six years ago where we were a fantastically good manufacturing organisation with a push out rather than an external focus starting with the shelf, and following the whole supply chain backwards. That is not how we did it. We were inefficient. The great basic service is about delivering what customers want, damage-free and on time, and we weren't very good at these five years ago. We had a measure of missed cases — availability was 96% and the number of missed cases 4%. We were probably delivering only two-thirds of our order on time. We weren't good enough."

The 4% of missed cases amounted to seven or eight million cases a year and cost P&G an estimated £40M. "We were losing a lot of money each year, so we put in place some big changes both in terms of the systems and processes that we had within the company and the physical infrastructure," says Poole.

As a result P&G invested in providing much greater capability in demand driven logistics — its ultimate aim — starting with synchronising the supply chain in line with consumer demand. "We invested over US$40M to upgrade our whole logistics infrastructure."

The changes included:
- Focusing on supplier relationship management and improving the speed and accuracy of information flow up the supply chain,
- Creating two distribution centres in the North and South to deliver the full range of P&G's ambient products on one truck.
- Introducing innovative schemes such as cross-docking so that products bypass storage, saving time and resources by going straight onto store shelves.
- Using IT solutions such as GPS tracking and electronic proof of delivery.

Reduced inventory

The transformation began with Procter & Gamble's physical infrastructure. It had three sites from which customers could order products — paper towels and nappies were produced at Manchester, laundry products at London and some toiletries at Skelmersdale — which forced customers to buy from three different places, rather than in line with demand. The group decided to give customers the opportunity to buy its whole ambient range from one place so that they could take advantage of efficient truckload ordering and ordering less quantity more often, enabling them to order much more in line with demand.

P&G also built a brand new automated distribution centre (DC) at its London plant at Dartford and upgraded its existing DC at Skelmersdale. Poole says that those changes alone had a drastic effect on the supply chain. He comments: "That was good because it meant there was fewer inventory in the total supply chain".

The group also recognised the advantages of enabling its larger customers to buy direct from the plants. Customers can go through the service centres and buy a truck full of anything they want. Also, for the physically big fast moving bulky items like nappies and soap powder they can order them direct from the plants.

Poole says: "We've done that to a certain extent already from our London and Manchester factories — London makes laundry products and Manchester makes nappies and kitchen towel — and we are extending that to other plants that are on the Continent." P&G is operating a two-tier distribution network which has drastically improved the basic service, says Poole.
Over the past 15 months the percentage of missed cases has reduced from 4% to less than 0.5%. However, Poole says that while there are still more opportunities for further improvement, the interventions made so far have led to a big change in the service provided. "The intervention that we made was critical, and that has given us the licence to get in and really work with customers more closely."

Collaborative planning

Poole says the development has helped better supply chain information synchronisation because the group is delivering to demand. Losses — reduced inventory and fewer truck miles — have been cut out of the supply chain. Having transformed the physical aspect of its supply chain, P&G turned its attention to having the right systems and processes in place so that it could collaborate with customers.

Changes here have included the creation of the Team Room, an area that has taken all the different disciplines of approach that the plants employ concerning day-by-day production, and applied it to a logistics environment, putting daily, weekly, monthly and annual processes in place and ensuring that everybody works on the right system in the first place. Poole says: "That was the other part of the jigsaw, and in the Team Room, one of the walls features the annual plan, strategies and where we are on each of those. We also have a daily meeting at 08.30 between all elements of the supply chain — the service centre, the DCs, the people that work with customers, the market planners and our order management people — so that everyone knows what happened yesterday, what's going to happen today and what needs to happen with customers."

Promotion forecasting was one area that had to be tackled and the Team Room has a board which highlights all the critical elements in putting together a big promotion. "Everyone can see whether things have been done or not." Poole says that a typical promotion can be for a physically big bulky product such as tissue towel for a supermarket chain. The number of cases involved could be at least 100,000. Poole cites another example where in the lead up to Christmas, he and his team had to ship cases of snack food Pringles to one of P&G's major customers. Poole says 150 x 40 foot trucks were used over the Christmas period.

P&G has also introduced joint forecasting within its supply chain. Poole explains: "Joint forecasting is about sitting down and agreeing quantities and delivery times together so that there are no surprises. With each of our customers we set up joint forecasting processes and for big customers and big promotions the forecasting detail — when they need it, how much is needed and delivery time — has to be signed off by the logistics and the commercial people on both sides, so that everybody knows what the deal is. The nightmares only come because there are surprises through lack of communication,"

Working with customers has improved P&G's service levels but, says Poole, the crusade continues. "Collaboration with customers is critical. You have to get in with the customers and understand what they want, working through the solution. Anything that improves service on shelf and reduces total supply chain costs from the factory gate outwards is up for grabs.

"What we don't want is to shunt value around the supply chain. We used to do that when customers had three sources to deal with — we were saying 'to get the best price you've got to order a truckload' and they would do that. What we were actually doing was washing our hands of it, and that wasn't good enough. All we did there was shunt the inventory and the problem onto another supply chain."

Poole stresses that companies have to sit down with customers and create a "logistics hit-list" highlighting the areas that will be mutually beneficial, improve service and reduce total supply chain costs: "That's the basis of our collaboration with any customer — let's work together to find the best way to improve service and reduce costs." In transforming its supply chain, P&G also approached major customers for input on improving its supply chain. "That's not to say we did everything they said," says Poole, "but we listened to them. And that's how it continues now. The collaboration work is based on what we can do to improve the flow of information up the supply chain; how we can make that faster and more accurate." Poole believes collaboration with customers is key to an efficient supply chain. He concludes: "A real focus on joint and collaborative planning with customers has been critical. It's all very well putting in great capability and structurally changing our supply chain but at the end of the day you can't make it happen unless you work with your customer."

Extracts from source: Logistics Manager June 2004

Type I and Type II supply chains: a contrast

As stated earlier, supply chains differ and the following model for two types of supply chain presents an "extremes" view to stimulate debate and discussion about the changes that may be needed. This is not intended to be a "good" or "bad" comparison.

The reality and the practice will be found in the "grey" between the "black/white" extremes; also, some aspects can be mixed between the two types. For example Type I on the main drivers and products; but Type II on inventory and buying etc.

Attribute	Type I Supply Chain Production led Push More about supply	Type II Supply Chain Market led Pull More about demand
Main driver	Forecast driven. Growth from volume output and ROI. Financial performance profit driven. "Pump" push. From Supply to demand. Mass production.	Order driven. Growth from customer satisfaction. Customer focus, value driven. "Turn on the Tap" pull. From demand to supply. Mass market.
Products	Launched. Functional, standard, commodities. Low variety. Long product life cycle.	Transition. Innovative, design and build, fashion goods. High variety. Short product life cycles.
Inventory	"Turns." Stock holding. Just in case. Hold safety stock. Seen as an asset/protection.	"Spins." Little stock holding. Just in time. No safety stock. Seen as a liability.
"Buying"	Buy goods for anticipated and projected demand/ needs. Instructed suppliers. Arms length, played off on a short term basis. Confrontation. Adversarial. Narrow range of suppliers. Low cost buying. Inspection on receipt.	Assign capacity on a daily basis. Involved suppliers. Committed suppliers, long term. Cooperation. Alliances. Ordered supplier base of specialists. Total acquisition cost buying. Quality assured.

"Making"	"Build." Proactive with orders. Economy of scale. Continuous flow and mass production. Long runs. Low production costs. High work in progress inventory. High plant efficiency e.g. 24/7. Labour is an extension of the machine. Ordered "push" schedules and reliable demand forecasts/make to stock.	"Supply." React to orders. Reduce waste. Batch, job shop, project methods of production, "customising". Short runs. Higher production costs. Low work in progress inventory. High effectiveness but with lower plant efficiencies. Labour brings the continuous improvements. Flexible "pull" Kanban schedules with make/assemble to order.
"Moving"	Move slower in bulk. Large/less frequent deliveries. Storage is high cost. Transport is a low cost. Fewer but larger RDC type deliveries.	Move faster in smaller quantities. Smaller, frequent deliveries. Storage is low cost. Transport costs are higher. Many varied and dispersed destinations.
Customers	Predictive demand.	Un-predictive demand.
	Cost driven. Are only handled at the top or by the "customer service" department.	Availability driven. Everybody is customer focussed.
Information	Demand information is sometimes passed back. Used mainly for "executing".	Demand information is mandatory. Used also for planning purposes.
Handling of Customers orders	10% forecast error and algorithmetic based forecasts. Continuous scheduled replenishment. More "push". Stock outs rarer (1-2%) and are dealt with contractually. Stable and consistent orders, some predictable weekly type ordering. Clear cut ordering. Service levels are more rigid.	40-100% error with forecasts more consultative based. Real time visibility throughout the supply chain. More "pull." Stock outs are immediate and frequent (10-40% p.a.) and volatile. Cyclical demand, many unpredictable orders. EDI/Visibility ordering. Service levels are more flexible to actual forecasts.
Deliver from stock lead times	Immediate, fast in one or two days.	Immediate to long; slower and from days to weeks.
Make to order lead times	1-6 months as mainly making "standard" products for stock.	1-14 days.

Costs	Mainly in physical conversion/movements. Inventory costs in finished goods. Cost control very strong and any gained savings are retained.	Mainly in marketing. Inventory costs in raw materials/wip. Revenue generation and any gained savings are shared.
Producer selling price	Low selling price. Few markdowns. 5-20% profits. Low risk.	Higher selling price. Many end of season markdowns. 20-60% profits. Higher risk levels.
Organisation methods	Silo/hierarchical management with some "cells". "Top down" to staff gives orders and responsibility. Professional managers who are more driven by power. Transactional/ownership. Self interest. Protective interfacing links. Slow to change, change is mainly resisted, and maintenance of the "status quo". Internal fragmentation with instructed employees. Tendency for "blame" cultures. "Fire-fighting" Little trust. People a liability and numbers are to be reduced wherever possible. Narrow skill base. Outside recruitment. "Do what you are told"	Flatter structures with cross functional teams. Top down and bottom up giving assistance; everyone is responsible. Leaders/educators who are people driven. Partnership/collaborative. Customer interest. Visible integrated links. Quicker response with continuous improvement and more embracive of change. "Joined up" structures with involved employees. More "gain" structure. "Fire-fighting" Extensive trust. People are an asset to be invested in. Multiple skill bases. Internal recruitment also. "Do what you think is best"

Finally in this section on understanding the supply chain and to link with section 2.0, please have a look at the following case study and specifically note the aspects of supply chain strategy.

Case Study: New Look (retail fashion and distribution)

Maintaining an efficient supply chain is a major priority for women's fashion retailer New Look in its ambitious plans for growth. The company is upgrading its stores and is widening its appeal beyond its traditional 16-24-year-old customers to older age groups, and needs the slickest possible logistics operation to support its strategy. Logistics director Alan Osborne has control of both inbound and outbound movements to maximise the smooth-running of the operation and to allow the company to respond quickly to the volatile fashion market. "That approach is absolutely critical in fashion.

Speed to market -from sheep to shop is fundamental," he says. The business strategy has already reaped benefits. Profit for the year to March 30 had more than doubled to £62.3m and by July sales revenues were up 12.3%. But the company has plans for further growth which the logistics department must support. Project Heartland aims to double overall retail floor space within five years to 200,000sq metres and will involve relocating stores to larger premises in key towns and cities -so far 41 stores have undergone the process with another 119 to go. The company is also refurbishing 300 smaller stores over two years in Project 300, intended to boost sales through existing space. Originally New Look had a strong southern bias and most of its stores were in south coast resort towns. This has changed as it has expanded and its distribution network has altered accordingly.

The company's main distribution centre, run in-house, is based at its Weymouth headquarters, where it has around 50,000sq m of warehouse space arranged over three floors. New Look is the town's largest employer and, at peak, 700 staff are employed in the distribution centre. "We have no plans to change that. We have a very loyal and reliable set of staff," Osborne says." The distribution centre is next to the buying office which is a great advantage. I am able to have regular contact with the buying and merchandising director and I am constantly talking to distribution centre staff as well."

However, the geographic shift in the business has made it necessary to use an additional facility in Doncaster to serve the North and Midlands. The warehouse opened last September and is owned and operated by P&O Trans European. Goods are trunked from Weymouth overnight and merged with those at Doncaster and sent out to the stores on New Look's fleet. Around 48% of the company's deliveries to stores are now made through the facility. P&O Trans European also uses the site for a contract with Flymo manufacturer Electrolux Outdoor Products.
As well as benefiting from shared over- heads, the two companies have different trading peaks and the, resources they use can be flexed accordingly. "There is a good mix of demand. They have a summer peak whereas we are more winter-based," Osborne says. This part of the operation was outsourced because New Look did not want to invest large amounts of capital in a distribution centre. "It was also a case of P&O having the resource available to allow us to make the move quickly," says Osborne.

As well as distribution to stores, New Look is paying a great deal of attention to inbound logistics. In future it intends to store more stock overseas, where storage costs are cheaper and use cross-docking when goods arrive in the UK. The company is setting up overseas consolidation centres for this purpose and one of these has opened in Greece, with another planned in Turkey.

Rather than packing single items, New Look is moving to ratio packs, where possible, to reduce handling. These contain several of the same garments in the most popular sizes — for example, packs might include a size 8, a 10, two 12s and a 14.
IT systems will play a major part in making the inbound operation work more

efficiently and Osborne says that the company will use fourth-party logistics. It is currently talking to the major providers about the work. "We'll be using a company with global representation. We want them to give us one systems solution so that we can have visibility of stock movements all around the world," Osborne explains.

Extracts from source: Motor Transport 29 August 2002

1.0. Action Time

For a company known to you

1. Construct a supply chain flow-chart/diagram/map (Note. Guidance notes, if required, on how to construct supply chain maps are included in section 4.0).

2. Compare and contrast this map with similar and dissimilar types of organisations.

3. The flows of information are often said to be as important as the flows of materials. Explain why this may be so, referring to your own or a business of your choice.

4. For the supply chain used above, assess the main strengths and weaknesses of this supply chain and the extent to which it provides competitive advantage for the business.

2.0. Supply Chain Planning

In this section we look at the following:

- Adopting a supply chain management approach
- Demand amplification
- Supply chain management strategy
- Supply chain and Traditional Accounting Practices
- Inventory
- Supply chain metrics
- Supply chain analysis
- Outsourcing
- Supply chain planning

Adopting a supply chain management approach

Many organisations (and supply chains) will need to change so that they can fully benefit from taking a total supply chain management approach. It is useful therefore to have some brief overviews of what may need to change:

From Traditional Ways >>>>>>>>>>>>>>>> To New Ways

Independence	Integration
Independent of next link	Dependency
Links are protective	End/end visibility
Means uncertainty	More certainty
Unresponsive to change	Quicker response
High cost, low service	High serve, lower cost
Fragmented internally	"Joined up" structures
Blame culture	"Gain" culture
Competing companies	Competing supply chains

The supplier/customer relationship can also change, for example:

From Interfacing< > < > < > < > < > < > < > To Integrating

Supplier Selection	Supplier Collaboration
Arms length	Total commitment
Confrontation and power based	Cooperation/collaboration
ay to day short term	Year to year and beyond
Clear cut ordering	EDI/Visibility
Transactional	Partnership/collaboration
Separated culture	Aligned cultures
Little trust	Extensive trust
Inspect and penalise	Quality assured

In turn this may mean changes in the following aspects:

Aspect	From	To	Means
Order Lot size	Large	Small	Reduced order
	Less frequent orders	More frequent orders	quantities
Suppliers	Multi sourcing	Single sourcing.	Fewer Suppliers.
	Short contract	Long term contracts.	Lower costs.
	Transactional		
	Rejects	No defects/Quality.	"Right first time"
	Low Price	Total Acquisition	
		cost.	Shared
	Arms length.	Collaboration	developments.
Scheduling	Suppliers	Buyers	Less variability
Lead Times	Long	Shorter	Less stocks

For many organisations, such changes may be onerous; therefore in summarising the benefits from taking a supply chain management approach, we can find the following options:

What needs to be done	The "do nothing" option
A few long term suppliers and joint action teams	Adversary, play offs with Suppliers
Short production runs with quick changeovers	Long product runs of products no longer needed
Minimal JIT Stockholding	"Just in case" expensive stock holding
Customers who are more demanding	Customers who get fed up, so go elsewhere
Right first time quality throughout	Inspections, reworking, warranty claims

Process & flatter cross functional management structures	Vertical, silo management structures
"Empowered", proactive "fire lighting" managers	"Turf conscious", reactive "fire fighting" managers
Continuous improvement and change	"Rowing the same boat but against the current" and resisting change

Demand amplification

The need for organisations to "Work Together" has been shown both internally and externally. If this is not done, then demand can be amplified as it passes down the chain (The "Forrester effect"). In a four player supply chain then the following will typically occur with the stock levels:

Factory	<<>>	**Distributor**	<<>>	**Wholesaler**	<<>>	**Retailer**
250		245		205		100

Note: these figures represent stock levels, being indexed at 100 with the retailer. So the multiple, for example at the factory end is times 2.5

This increase in stock and the "bullwhip" effect is explained by the following diagram, where, each player is holding safety stock as a protection from both the uncertainty in supply and, or demand:

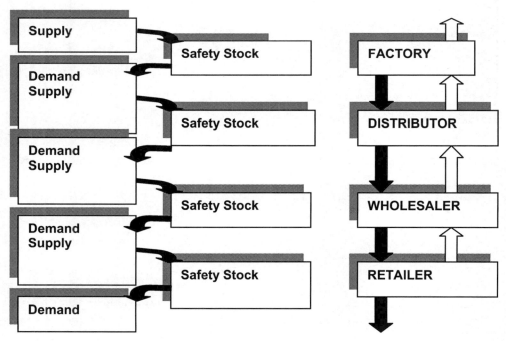

The ways to overcome this increase in stock holding in the supply chain are as follows:
- Improve information flows (e.g. become demand driven)
- Improve supply goods flows (e.g. 3PL milk rounds e.g. kitting)
- Remove the commercial obstacles and link together in a different way (e.g. by cost transparency, performance contracts, demand drivers)
- Recognise any blocks remaining and arrange/agree for contingency cover (e.g. contingency stocking)
- Work together as one (e.g. relationship development; people/team management across the chain and not just within companies)

All the above four players need to integrate, coordinate and control together. For example, the factory, distributor and wholesaler must have visibility of the retailers end demand and work together collaboratively.

This effect has been shown above in a single supply chain. Imagine the impacts on, the common reality of, multiple level supply chains and networks.

Demand Replenishment in networks

Most players in supply chain management have multiple levels of supply chain involvement. Therefore managing inventory in a sequential and simple supply chain is different, to that found when having to manage inventory across multiple level supply chains; for example within a distribution network, or across many different players. The following shows some of these differences:

Key Area	Simple supply chain	Multiple supply chain
Objective for inventory levels	Incremental view per DC/stock holding place	Total view across the supply chain
Demand forecasts	Independent at each level	Based on end customer
Lead times	Work on first level suppliers lead time and variability	Use all/ holistic lead times
Forrester effects	Ignored, "not my problem"	Measured and allowed for in replenishment planning
Visibility	To first level supplier and customer only	Holistic visibility
Customer service	Differentiation is not possible	Differentiation is possible
Cost implications	Incremental costs giving high holistic cost levels	Modelled for optimisation across the supply chain

Meanwhile, the following case study illustrates demand amplifications and the Forrester effect:

Case Study: Forrester Effect

In this case, the information ripples backward through the delivery process to create havoc at the production end of the chain.

Megadrug is a well-established pharmaceutical company. It has a wide range of products distributed over the world. One of its newer products is a homeopathic drug, Homeocold, to stop colds from evolving into real nastiness. Megadrug supplies retail shops from various regional centres. In March last year, at the end of the winter season, orders from retailers unexpectedly started to pour in. The regional centres serviced the shops and ordered the plant for more Homeocold. Unfortunately, the production line at the plant had already been switched to another 'summer' drug, and it would take at least a week before Homeocold could be produced again.

As the regional centres stocked out, the retailers were frantically ordering more Homeocold. Megadrug's management team realised then that a media-triggered 'poisonous drugs' scare had resulted in millions of customers switching from traditional drugs to homeopathic alternatives. After a crisis meeting, they decided to switch production back to Homeocold in order to service the increasing backlog with the regional centres. Even at full production for one month, they would not be able to catch up; but one thing Megadrug could not afford was a reputation for unreliability with retailers and customers.

Weeks later, the regional centres finally started servicing the retailers again. To their surprise, they were greeted with relief at first, but, as the weeks went by, with embarrassment. Retailers started cancelling orders, faster and faster. The regional centres, watching piles of Homeocold accumulate in their warehouses, started screaming at the plant to stop producing and shipping Homeocold.

The plant director was pulling out his last remaining strands of hair. He was now asked to stop producing Homeocold and to catch up with the summer production that had got way behind schedule. The management team was too busy blaming each other to notice that Homeocold was still selling steadily more than usual and decided to delay production next year to get rid of the stocks at the regional centres. By increasing expectations and ignoring the obvious delays involved, the company faced a "Forrester effect". Minor market changes at the end of the supply chain accumulated to cause great havoc with production planning. Once again not reacting would have been safer than over-reacting.

Source: Balle, Systems Thinking

Supply chain management strategy

The strategic aspects basically involve an organisation considering and deciding on, "how we will win." It also requires an awareness of the expected development of the business in terms of the future:

- Product; format, volumes, through-puts and new product development
- Inventory; format, holding/levels, locations
- Suppliers; purchasing methods and locations of supply
- Production; methods and location of production sites
- Physical distribution; methods and locations of warehouses/DCs
- Customers; marketing methods and locations of customers/product destinations

Mission – Vision

Having a mission for the supply chain will assist the strategic direction. From the discussion so far in this book, it is possible to view that the mission of supply chain management is:

- Transparent flows
- Flexibility
- A share to gain approach
- A reliance on quality
- Elimination of all barriers to all the internal and external activities
- Elimination of inventory whilst optimally balancing costs, service levels and availability
- Timely delivery to customers

The following case shows how one companies' used a vision to integrate a supply chain:

Case Study: Import Logistics - Asda's Vision and supply chain integration

Spending -1997- £1200 million on imports via third party wholesalers and £500 million on direct imports.

Previously:
- No systems
- No cost visibility
- Used middlemen
- No economy of scale
- Poor product availability

 - For example, home and leisure products ordered through UK agents who arranged everything.

 - For example, beers, wines and spirits bought ex works or fob and arranged through 4 forwarders.

Internal Structure fragmented:
- Trading on product selection, negotiations, selection of suppliers, and ordering
- Finance on letters of credit, payments
- Logistics on order quantity and phasing into supply chain
- Treasury on buying currency

Determined "Import Vision":
- To establish supply chain control
- To provide full cost visibility
- To maximise economies of scales in both product and in freight buying
- To outsource non core activities
- To deliver a credible import capability

The solution:
- Tender and then outsource to one forwarder
- Asda maintains and determines carrier selection as appropriate
- Freight costs fell by 8 per cent
- Duty charges reduced by 10 per cent
- Fuller visibility of supply chain
- Centralised the previous fragmented internal control

Sources: Supply Management 9 April 1998 and Logistics Manager Jan/Feb 1998

It will be seen that the vision effectively gave direction towards the solution.

Supply chain and Traditional Accounting Practices

Finance is an important element for most organisations where the generally accepted accounting principles create the foundation for all organisations to report financial data in the same way. Such principles have a long history, for example, back to the early days of industrialisation. This long history however, has meant that accounting rules have not always kept up with current business practices.

Whilst this has been recognised and has resulted in some new accounting methods (for example Activity Based Costing), profit/loss and balance sheets statements do still reflect traditional historic accounting practices and do not reflect current global supply chain practises.

Some differences between supply chain management and accounting have been noted as follows:

	Supply Chains	Accounting
Process	Horizontal flows across different organisations and functions.	Vertical transactions within one "silo" in an organisation.
Focus	External with suppliers and contractors and customers/consumers.	Internal looking and within organisational boundaries.
Time	Ongoing flows of products and information. For example, inventory turnover and lead times performances impact the financial figures, but are not reported in company accounts	Period reporting causes disconnects. For example, inventory is reported on the balance sheet annually but the warehouse holding costs appear monthly in the cost accounts
Perspective	Dynamic and changing. Forward looking.	Static and historical. Backward looking.

Based on source: Tom Craig http://www.ltdmgmt.com/mag/index.html

In view of these differences, it is important that supply chain management ensure they understand how financial accounting practices work, as these will most certainly have an impact on the organisational decision making.

Importance of Finance in the Supply Chain

Finance is the management of money and in the UK involves capitalism which means using capital (money and profits) in a market economy that involves customers, sales and the exchange of money.

Supply chain alternatives can and do enable optimisation of a corporate goal for profit maximisation. For example:

- Inventory minimisation may be needed due to the competing needs for capital and the difficulty many firms have in raising capital.
- Various cost levels of customer service can be analysed to find the most profitable level for an organisation.

Profit and loss

All the supply chain activities contribute to the make up of the cost of goods sold (COGS). The following diagram, taken from *Emmett & Granville (2007)* shows how this process takes place and identifies the competitive variables and the supply chain variables that influence the profit and loss (revenue and cost).

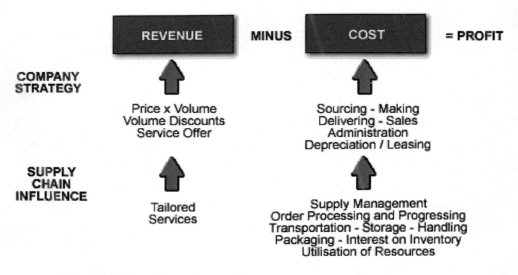

Revenue is the total sales in financial terms that an organisation makes.

Cost is the total cost in financial terms, which is attributable to that year's trading. Profit can then be obtained from the following calculation:

Revenue - Cost = Profit.

In reality the profit here would be referred to as operating profit. There would still be interest to pay on any money borrowed for the business, for example from a bank. Once this charge has been removed then the final figure given is the contribution. There would also be a tax on this figure fixed by a countries fiscal authority. For annual company accounts, the above process can be seen within the "Profit and Loss" statement.

However, if the costs were more than the revenue our profit would be negative, demonstrating a loss; hence the term "Profit and Loss". Company strategy can influence many variables that are seen on the profit and loss account. Price, for example, if increased whilst unit sales stay the same, will drive up revenue. If a discounting strategy is adopted, numbers of units sold may increase but revenue may drop for the business. Additionally, one of the biggest drivers of revenue is the overall customer service package on offer.

The organisations profit and loss account covers a given period of time, usually one year. Providing the sale of the item and the purchase of the materials to make it, occur in the same period, both the revenue and cost will occur in the profit and loss statement. When however material is purchased in one time period and then is used in a later period and adjustment has to be made to the profit to allow for the increase in stock levels.

Balance Sheet

The balance sheet of the company shows the financial worth of the company at a specific point in time.

In addition to revenue and cost as drivers of profit/loss, there are other factors to be taken into account, which have a critical impact on corporate financial performance. These are:
- Fixed assets
- Current assets
- Liabilities

1) Fixed Assets
Assets are things that can be sold for cash. Fixed assets are things owned like building/pre plant and equipment. There values are listed as a fixed asset on the balance sheet.

2) Current Assets
Customers who owe money are debtors are current assets as they can be turned into cash hopefully as soon as possible. Stock is also a current asset so they have a value and will th on the balance sheet. Also if there is cash in the bank this will be recorded as a current a

3) Current Liabilities
These are third parties that are owed money (creditors). Examples here are supplier not yet been paid for the goods they have delivered or a bank overdraft.

4) Long term liabilities; for example, long term loans.
In addition, the balance sheet includes share capital or shareholders funds. Those put money into the business or have since invested in the business and are owed return on that money. Also, reserves and retained profit; the profit kept from p reinvest in the business.

As the assets must equal the liabilities or "Balance" this statement is referred to as the Balance Sheet. Again the supply chain impact can be seen in the following diagram:

ASSETS	LIABILITIES
FIXED ASSETS	**CURRENT LIABILITIES**
	Trade creditors
Propert, plant and equipment	Overdraft
	SHAREHOLDERS'
Own or lease distribution Facilities, equipment?	**FUNDS**
	Share Capital
	Reserves
Storage, transportation and systems choices?	Return to shareholders?
CURRENT ASSETS	**LONG TERM LIABILITIES**
Cash - Liquidity Inventory - stock	Return on total investment

...rant to see how a revenue and cost statement and balance sheet can work over a ...d of time.

...low

...ply chain flows of goods and materials, the flows of cash money are critical. A ...ofitable yet, what if it runs out of cash then it cannot pay suppliers or wages ...will mean that there is then no business. Managing cash flow is therefore

s appear   ...ipts)
set.   ...ents)
                 ...int of cash, available, at the right time

that have   ...lows:

	g the Out
who initially	g things
money or a	...s
...evious years to	...it

...ill need a short term loan/overdraft at an extra cost

Consequently cash flow management means answering the following questions:
• How much cash is needed?
• What is the balance between in or out?
• When is it needed?

Cash flow and Profit

Profit results for making sales, less the costs. This is known as operating profit. Profit is therefore assessed at the time of sale and not at the time of payment. In turn, cash comes from when the receipts (in) exceed the payments (out). Accordingly profit is not cash, as they are separated/linked by time. Consider the following simple example:

Ordered and delivered by a supplier in March, customer pays at the end of May and payment is received early June by the supplier. Profit is assessed in March, but cash is not received until early June.

It will be seen therefore that the flows of goods and materials have different impacts to the cash flows of all organisations. Cash flow or 'funds flow' is concerned with the amount of cash available in the business at any one time. This is a very important part of operating a business. For example, a business may make a good profit but if it doesn't have cash available to pay the monthly interest to the bank or to pay suppliers, then it will fail.

To manage cash flow, the following options are used:

• Supplier looks to delay payments to its own suppliers (creditors) or obtain longer credit terms; for example from 30 to 60 days.
• Suppliers examine credit levels given to its customers (debtors); for example from 60 to 30 days.
• Reduce stock levels.
• Lease facilities and in-company transport equipment thus releasing capital.
• Suppliers examine the time it takes to convert materials during production.

This is summarised in the following diagram:

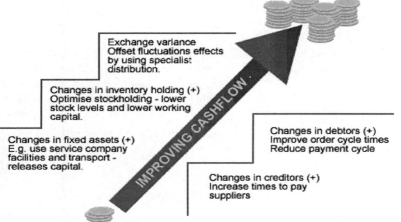

57

Return on Investment

Most organisations aim to give the best return possible to their shareholders. However, the majority aim to do this in order to retain their investors' money in the business, so they can continue operating and even attract new investors who can lend them money to grow or expand their businesses. The key attraction is, if the business can give an investor a larger return, than if the investor had simply put the money in the bank for a nominal interest payment.

A future investor may want to know how much money they will see on a £100 investment in the company in a year's time. Another way of looking at it, is what return the investor would get on the capital employed (£1) in the business over one year.

The capital employed can be used in financial measures. For example, profit divided by the capital employed will give a common measure of the return on capital employed (ROCE). If, for example, the investor puts £1 into a business; the business makes a profit of £25,000 and has capital employed of £100,000 the ROCE will be 1:4 or 25%. If bank interest is 10% then the investor will get a good return. The process can be seen diagrammatically:

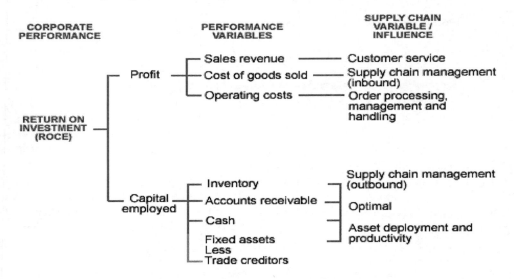

It is clear that in order to improve corporate financial performance the profit needs to be larger. By improving customer service within the supply chain sales can be helped to grow. By managing the supplier product costs (COGS) and keeping operating costs down, the profit can be increased. There is also an argument for leasing company vehicles, equipment and facilities as this will reduce the capital employed and increase the ROCE. Similarly, by reducing debtors and lengthening times to pay creditors, the overall capital employed will go down. Within companies the statements "Get things moving and moving fast" and "sweat your assets" come from this philosophy.

The ROCE can also be referred to as return on investment (ROI).

Other measures investigated are profit margin (profit/sales) and capital turnover (sales/capital employed). As shown below when multi-plied together they equal ROCE:

$$\frac{Profit}{Sales} \; X \; \frac{Sales}{Capital\;Employed} = \frac{Profit}{Capital\;Employed}$$

We know that the supply chain has an indirect impact on sales as improved service tends to lead to better sales. From the equation above we can see therefore that the supply chain has an indirect impact on profit and hence profit margin. However, the supply chain also has a direct impact on capital employed and therefore, capital turnover or asset turnover. The supply chain has therefore, a very powerful multi-plicative impact on margin. If capital employed is reduced by 50% then our ROI will double.

Inventory

Inventory as seen above, is a current asset in finance terms and is also used to generate cash from selling product for profit. The flows of goods and information will need coordinating to minimise the inventory levels that, as noted earlier, can often be viewed as the main "poorly" symptom of a supply chain, and therefore needs "treatment". Inventory is also the common component throughout the Supply Chain, either as raw material, sub assemblies/work in progress or as finished goods (which are often held at multiple places in the supply chain). It can also be the "knock on" from one player to another player, as seen earlier in the Forrester effect. To prevent such effects, "one number" views at individual SKU levels in the forecasts and orders are required through the supply chain.

Inventory is therefore an important component to understand. Also, any changes in the supply chain structuring will inevitably have impacts on where and how much inventory is being held. The format of inventory and where it is held is therefore of common interest to all supply chain players and must be jointly investigated and examined.

Inventory management is an approach to manage the product flow in a supply chain, to achieve the required service level at an acceptable cost. Movement and product flow are key concepts as when the flow stops, then cost will be added (unless the stored product is one that appreciates in value over time).

Key aspects that are to be considered in inventory management are:

- Determining the products to stock and the location where they are held.
- Maintaining the level of stock needed to satisfy the demand (by forecasting of demand).
- Maintaining the supply.
- Determining when to order (the timing).
- Determining how much to order (the quantity).

The supply chain is all about satisfying demand; this will be found in two basic forms: **Independent** or **random demand** is independent of all other products; for example, a tyre

manufacturer, for puncture repairs. Independent demand has the following characteristics:
- is the direct consumer driven demand for products or services.
- is more random with uncertainty being found.
- uses re-order point/level systems for inventory management/replenishment.

Dependant or **predicative demand** is that derived after consumer demand for "end use" products or services and has the following characteristics:
- is driven by the derived demand requirement (for example, a tyre manufacturer supplying tyres for new cars to a car assembler, and is planned for by the car assembler, based on their view of the independent demand from consumers).
- this means that the previous event has to happen first and that subsequent events will then depend on the ones preceding them.
- is therefore more certain for suppliers enabling some degree of anticipation (for example, the tyre manufacturer, obtains from the car assemblers their forward planning on production).
- uses requirement/resource planning systems (MRP) for inventory management/replenishment.

Inventory and uncertainty

A key aspect of inventory management is dealing with uncertainty. This can be found in both the supply and also with the customer/consumer demand. But it is always necessary to ask whether such uncertainty is "real" (and is definitely caused by the dynamic aspects of the supply chain), or is it caused by institutionalised and out-dated/ill-informed procedures and lack of communication between the supply chain players.

An example here is with the earlier mentioned Forrester effect, when institutionalised demand distorts the real demand as the demand passes down a supply chain with each player viewing the demand as being random.

This can cause fluctuations and dependencies that can limit subsequent events occurring as these depend on the last previous dependencies and are therefore being influenced by the fluctuations of the preceding dependencies. Where the supply chain is long with no end to end visibility, the length of dependencies in turn, increase, meaning higher inventory carrying and slower movement as each dependency struggles to undertake its activities due to the fluctuations. They struggle with the capacity as the demand and the flow are not in balance.

Inventory Costs

These are caused by many aspects; consider for example the "external" costs that accrue from any Forester effects. The cause of these costs comes from many different "internal" activities and departments of a company; furthermore, many of the costs may be hidden from view.

The following cost items can be involved:

Capital Investments:
- Value of Stock holding.
- Warehouse investment.
- Warehouse equipment investment.
- ICT systems investments.

Plus...Product holding costs
- Storage/handling (if not in above) .
- Obsolescence.
- Deterioration /damages to stock.
- Insurance.

Plus...Ordering costs
- Purchasing.
- Warehouse receiving.
- Finance payments.

All these individual cost items equal the total cost of inventory where, the Total Cost of Inventory is as follows:

Total of Capital investment @ Cost of borrowing money per annum
+ Holding total costs per annum,
+ Ordering costs per annum,
+ Any other, specific annual costs

As an example of total inventory cost, a large multi-national oil company indicates the following percentage costs of its inventory value per annum:

Physical storage	3-5%
Deterioration /obsolescence	2%
Opportunity cost (cost of capital tied up)	12-23%
Total inventory costs	**17-30%**

Inventory Service

This centres around the level needed (the availability), to satisfy demand. This will usually be a strategic decision of the business, but it can also be a decision taken at a lower level to provide cover against complaints and "noise" factors. Inventory is a dynamic and interactive process, and such anti "noise" low level decision making can be reflections that inventory it is not fully understood and that sub-optimal decision making is occurring in the business.

The levels of stock being held to satisfy demand should be a company strategic policy decision based upon an objective view of the requirements of users and customers. In a market situation, what the competition is offering will also have an input into such strategic decisions.

Inventory and Lead Time

Lead time has been looked at earlier. It is a critical component in making inventory decisions; as the following simple example illustrates:

If the use is 70 items per week, and the supply LT is 2 weeks: then the maximum stock is 140 items.

But if the supply LT is variable by +/- one week, then, the maximum stock is 210 items and the minimum stock is 70 items - people may decide to play it safe and hold 210 items. This is not the best decision but maybe an understandable one for those who are left to base replenishment decisions on protecting against personal "noise" factors when past stock outs have occurred. In such cases, then clearly inventory management is also not understood or involved both strategically and operationally in the business.

For those wishing to explore inventory more fully, it is fully covered in *"Excellence in Inventory Management"* by Emmett and Granville (2007).

Planning Inventory

Meanwhile the following Model and Rules are used to show what is required, so that inventory is correctly planned for:

Model for Planning Inventory

1. Establish whether current performance is cost or service driven

2. Conduct an ABC/Pareto analysis and demand analysis
*   E.g. focus on the important few not the trivial many

3. Consider reducing order quantity options
*   E.g. reorder only enough to cover demand until next receipt

4. Measure and consider reducing safety stock
*   E.g. hold only when protects service against variable demand
*   E.g. Supply lead time and variability examination
*   E.g. check service levels are needed
*   E.g. review levels
*   E.g. measure and improve forecast accuracy
*   E.g. reduce number of stockholding locations

5. Reduce finished goods stocks
*   E.g. move towards make/assemble to order
*   E.g. reduce variations, obsoletes, low sale items
*   E.g. make smaller batches

6. Review and check parameters manually and regularly, the target being zero inventories
- E.g. Analysis at item level
- E.g. order more frequently at item level

7. Aim for short fixed lead times with accurate demand forecasting

Seven Rules for Inventory Management

1. All inventories should be justified, and, minimised with the target being zero inventory.

2. Staff will need training and motivating to correctly identify, locate and count all inventory correctly.

3. Safety stock should only be held to protect variable demand to give customer service, or, against variable supply lead times.

4. Orders should only be placed when a stock out is anticipated.

5. Re-order just enough to cover demand, until the next receipt is due.

6. Focus effort on the few important items and not on the trivial many.

7. ICT can help and take away the "number crunching", but manual checks and reviews are still needed.

Outsourcing

As part of supply chain planning, it may prove useful to concentrate on core activities and outsource the non core. Outsourcing is often therefore a strategic direction. The following "secrets" have been identified by "Supply Management" (29 June 2000):

- Concentrate of what do well and allow specialists in other areas to handle the non core services
- Adapt to new ideas and developments, as, what was acceptable in the past, may not be so in the future
- Choose a provider who understands all your needs
- It is crucial to fully know your current costs/service level
- Ensure outsourcing delivers, planned benefits such as cost/service/time targets
- Acknowledge that information equals power in areas such as service level requirements
- Develop a strategic partnership with the provider, based on mutual trust
- Start with a phase controlled service with monitored cost/service levels at all stages
- Develop the right company culture which supports outsourcing
- Monitor the outsource function with performance measurement regularly

Many activities can be outsourced , from general cleaning and catering services to specific supply chain activities like distribution (transport, warehousing), purchasing and production. Indeed for many years, UK retailers such as Marks & Spencer have not manufactured any of the products which carry their brand name.

Similarly many of the road freight vehicles, seen delivering goods from a named producer that is shown/advertised on the vehicle, are often being operated by a third party company, to who the named producer has outsourced the transport.

The following questions can be used to help start in the thinking process on whether to outsource:

- Are your objectives achievable with outsourcing?
- Are the suppliers available to perform at least your current expectations?
- Have you any agreements that limit your capability to outsource?
- What exactly do you want to outsource? For example with distribution; the physical handling in your retained premises with your equipments (basically a managed labour service supply), through to the whole operation including transport delivery, (involving also the provision of all warehouse and transport assets)?

The following also provides a view on whether to outsource:

- Is the activity a non-core one? Whatever the answer, Management control must remain a core activity, as should, customer contact.
- Can we release some capital? For example with 3 Party distribution, they have low return on capital employed (ROCE) ratios, typically 10 per cent, probably well below that expected by some other companies/sectors.
- Will we retain some operations in house? It may be useful to do this for cost comparisons and service benchmarking.
- Will we retain Management expertise? This is important to do; companies should never fully sub contract control.
- What increased monitoring will be needed? This should be the same as is currently done, but there is often a need to especially watch closely the customer service standards.
- What are the risks of committing to one outsourced contractor? Flexibility in the contract maybe possible, alternatively multi-sourcing could be the answer.
- Will flexibility be increased? It should be flexible as in theory, as the outsourcing company can maybe divert non-specialised resources elsewhere, as after all, the service they are perfoming, is their core business.
- Will costs be reduced, whilst service increased? This is the ideal.
- How will we account for future changes? Presumably the same as without the contractor; but contract term and 'get outs' is the issue to be considered here.
- Are there any Transport of Undertaking Protection of Employees legislation (TUPE) implications? There probably will not be if there are less than 5 people, or, some direct control is retained of key operations, or, if relocated. There probably will be if the assets or, the whole business is being transferred. (Legal advice will be needed to determine the "probably" impacts).

Meanwhile, profitable and successful companies that provide outsourced services are reported to be those that have:

- Created an open dialogue and understood customers needs.
- Priced according to the resources used and/or the value delivered.
- Been open on providing productivity measurements.
- Use the appropriate technology.
- Demonstrate flexibility.
- Desire to implement change and best practice.

Supply chain planning

The focus should always be towards customers, internal or external. It should always be recalled that supply chain management is all about the horizontal flow of goods/materials, information and money. This movement will usually be across often vertical and bureaucratic functional silos. The horizontal flows and the vertical management silos will need to be integrated so that coordination of the flows are realised; for outcomes like growth, lower costs, improved service etc.

From a strategic and tactical point of view, this will mean:

- restructuring internal organisational relationships, for example, with the earlier mentioned cross functional management structure.
- market evaluation.
- identifying different customer segments requiring individual supply/demand chains.
- developing synchronised relationships with suppliers and customers.
- implementing the enabling ICT.

Main areas in SCM

The five main areas that affect the supply chain in any organisation will be as follows:

1) Supply Chain (s) Configuration
What and where are the de-coupling points, e.g. the places where to buy, make, move, and sell? It is more than likely that the current configurations will be wrong, as different products and different customers require different supply chains. Also, the required performance levels will differ. Therefore, fundamental decisions are needed about what gets done, how it gets done, and where it gets done, for these different supply chains.

2) Management practices
What are the processes and practices that facilitate "buy, make, move, and sell?"

When where these last examined and improved?

How open is the organisation to quickly change?

- For example, joint planning, and objectives with suppliers and customers on KPIs covering service, cycle times flexibility and stock levels

- For example, joint product development, strategic supplier relationships, vendor managed inventory
- For example, centralised stock holding, moving direct with single handling
- For example, in Europe, using assemble/pack to order planning and operations

3) Relationships
How are suppliers and customers aligned?
- With suppliers, these can include, close collaboration with extensive information sharing to total outsourcing
- With customers, these can include becoming the preferred supplier/partner

Building such relationships involves time, patience, commitment, and ultimately, trust. Companies will usually only do these, when they have a clear business strategy and clear core competencies. Courage and self-confidence then enables strategic relationships to be formed.

4) Organisation
How are cross-functional tasks and decisions carried out and undertaken?
Internal organisation and structure is critical. Accountability and authority for the entire supply chain(s) is best wherever possible.
- If products are unique, then reporting in to the appropriate business unit may be used
- If portions of the supply chain are shared, then ownership maybe in accordance with the functional organisation, for example localised or globalised

Above all, what needs to happen is aligned performance objectives from end to end and aligned decision making authority from end to end.

5) Information communication technology
- How is ICT used to support the integrated supply chain?
- ICT is often the enabler for supply chain management improvement. It should not however be used in isolation of all the above

Strategic Design

The points arising from these five main areas mean that Supply Chains will need a strategic design to cover the following aspects:

1) Customer Demand
- Design the supply chain on market needs-as it is demand that "kick starts" the whole process
- Understand the supply chain requirement for customer segments,(and tailor as appropriate)

2) Product
- Will vary, for example: standard, segmented standard, customised standard, tailored customised, pure customised

- Design products for interchange ability, ease of assembly, and standardised parts
- Assemble to order, customised products
- Postpone final product differentiation until the product is required

3) Strategic direction

- Need a top recognition and commitment to the supply chain purpose/vision that recognises, it is fundamental to integrate independent processes for interdependency
- Concentrate on areas that have maximum business impact
- Leverage e-business to link assets and process, across partners
- Minimise fixed costs, keeping assets and resources flexible
- As supply chains are collections of business that add value, focus on the core value drivers. Then perform more added value work
- Outsource non strategic and non competitive activity (DIY or Buy In)
- Adopt and enforce common performance and quality standards throughout the supply chain
- Use flow logistics by designing all processes for the continuous flow of goods and information, therefore minimising lead times and stockholding
- Design and manage adaptable supply chain networks
- Manage through a cross functional organisation and structure
- Appreciate flexible relationships across the supply chain
- Continually develop the people , so that they will continuously improve
- Remember that supply chains may appear to be technically simple, but remain managerially difficult

All the above decisions involve capital and risk, for example:
- Which products to sell?
- How many production plants?
- Which suppliers?
- What to stock and how much?
- What distribution network?
- Which of the above to make/buy in, or, do self/outsource?

The following case study shows some aspects of strategic planning undertaken in Halfords supply chain.

Case Study: Halfords Supply Chain

A large number of stores, a wide product range and sharp seasonal peaks- Halfords have some serious logistical challenges to face. And, to meet the needs of the business, the company has undergone a comprehensive supply chain review.

This has covered inbound logistics, warehouse operations, renewal of the fleet and IT systems. It started around two years ago, with implementation beginning last year, and is still continuing. Running through it is a desire to support the operation of the retail outlets as effectively as possible and to boost revenue.

Operations controller Steve Nicholls says: "It's all focused on improving the availability of products in the stores and increasing sales, while at the same time reducing our investment in stock."

Locations

Halfords is owned by CVC Capital Partners which bought the company from Boots last September. It has more than 400 stores spread around the country, three-quarters of them in out-of-town locations with the remainder in high streets and motorway service areas. Its products include car parts, car accessories such as audio systems, bicycles and cycling accessories. This in itself creates a large range of products for the distribution network to handle but the number of lines has been widened by its Arcade trading format, which is now fully up and running in 160 stores.

Specialist

In the stores that have been converted there are separate and distinct areas for certain products with specialist sales assistants and an extended product range-for example "Rip speed" for car enhancement and "Bike hut" for two-wheeled transport. The network has also had to cope with growth of the chain in recent years of around 15 stores a year. The seasonal sales fluctuations Halfords has to manage include volumes of cycles, which can treble at Christmas and then increase again in the summer, and de-icers and screen washers, which can rise dramatically in the autumn.

Halfords has three distribution centres supporting the business. The largest of these, known as Washford, is co-located at the company's/head office in Redditch/and handles small such as car parts, which are picked into plastic trays, and the majority of larger items, which are transported in roll cages. A second Redditch warehouse, called Lakeside, handles cycles and bulky items such as roof boxes for cars.

These depots are supported by the third facility at Cowley in Oxfordshire which stores both smaller and larger items, most of them lines with a predictable sales pattern. The goods are trunked to Redditch and consolidated with the products from the other two warehouses, before being sent out to the stores. The Cowley depot is run by Unipart but the other two are warehouses operated in-house. The transport linking the depot network and the stores is contracted out to TDG. The dedicated fleet of 40 vehicles is a mixture of articulated vehicles, used to serve the out-of-town stores, and five draw-bars which are used to serve Halfords' high street stores.

Flexibility

Nicholls says that the main advantages of using a third party for transport are the operational flexibility that it brings and the ability to cope with both the technological aspects of running a fleet and the frequent changes in regulations.

"We are able to call on considerable expertise within TDG and, because they have an on-site management team, we have daily contact as well as regular meetings,' he says. One instance of this cooperation is in the creation of double-deck trailers, which are being jointly developed by Halfords, TDG and trailer manufacturer Montracon, to serve the stores. They will be able to combine deliveries from the two Redditch warehouses and thereby cut costs.

Warehouse
Currently most stores receive separate deliveries from the two facilities - the new Arcade stores receive four deliveries a week, two from each warehouse, while the rest of the chain receives two, one from each warehouse. As the changes to the supply chain are introduced, Halfords should have the capacity to increase the deliveries to the stores and thereby become more responsive to customer demand. "One of the main aims of the changes we are bringing in is to increase the frequency of deliver" Nicholls says.

Halfords has been trialling the new trailers for two years but is now in a position to use them on a more widespread basis. This month it is taking delivery of two batches of 12, bringing the total to 36 double-deckers.

The new trailers' suspension has a lifting mechanism which raises them to a standard dock height of 1.2m. Meanwhile some of the docks in the Washford warehouse have been excavated so that when the vehicles reverse up to the warehouse the upper deck is level with the floor of the warehouse.

At the same time as introducing the double-deckers Halfords has replaced some of its tractors with Volvo units containing the Dynafleet installation which it is using to improve vehicle performance in conjunction with driver training. Currently stores are served on a milk round system of fixed delivery times that allows them to know within a half-hour window when their deliveries will arrive during the week. However, Halfords is considering the possibility of using dynamic scheduling to maximise vehicle utilisation but this would only take place after the company's overall IT and communications systems have been upgraded.

Installation
The operation of the warehouses is also being improved through the of Manhattan system which it is using to Associates' PKMS warehouse improve warehouse management system this summer. This will replace the companies existing in house warehouse system. "It will be a lot more flexible and will result in an increase in picking accuracy," Nicholls says.

As well as the operational enhancements Halfords is introducing, it is improving its environmental performance in the supply chain, as part of an overall company policy that includes recycling of packaging cardboard from the stores and the depots. "We have the sort of reverse logistics you would expect from a company of our size. We are extending our packaging waste collection system at the moment and already use reusable transit cases in our operation wherever we can;' Nicholls explains.

Source: Motor Transport 27 March 2003

2.0. Action Time: Media Consumer Products PLC

Media Consumer Products PLC (MCP) is a large wholesale distributor of home entertainment products, supplying many of Britain's best-known retailers with 45% of the UK music and DVD/video industry's entire output.

"The broad mix of products and throughputs made this a very challenging industry," commented the supply chain manager at MCP. "Inventory is a major part of our costs, so order accuracy, product protection and the accuracy of our stock management are all critical factors for our business."

With the ability to unite the interests of suppliers and retailers, it makes it attractive, simple and profitable for them to all do business together. MCP clients are major supermarkets/other retail outlets, along with supplying the fulfilment to many on-line portal companies.

The MCP warehouse provides reliable, efficient movement and tracking of product from receipt, through appropriate storage and picking systems, to sortation and dispatch. MCP has developed automated handling systems to deliver exceptional 99.9 per cent order accuracy from their NDC. To handle the rapid growth in MCP's business the NDC has been designed to provide a flexible expansion path to accommodate a throughput of up to 150 million items a year, while supporting an increase in the number of SKUs.

The entertainment industry is unusual in having a very large number of both suppliers and products, with the most popular 10 per cent of titles accounting for more than 95 per cent of throughput. This 10 per cent is, however, extremely dynamic, with around 200 changes each week, and new items ('chart toppers') frequently coming in with an exceptionally pronounced volume spike.

To meet the business requirements efficiently, the NDC integrated operations that are optimised for five different levels of throughput.
- Super-fast items
- Fast movers
- Medium movers
- Slow moving items.
- Very slow moving items

Task
1. What do you believe should be the MCP supply chain strategy
2. Give advice on the pattern and the requirements for inventory, in the MCP supply and demand chains?

3.0. Supply Chain Operations

After reading this section you will be better able to understand:

*   Procurement
*   Production
*   Physical distribution
*   Marketing
*   Supply chain performance and key performance indicators
*   Benchmarking
*   Contingency planning

Introduction

Within each component/functional process of the supply chain (buying, making, moving and selling), specific aspects can be found that will assist in supply chain optimisations. These "what is done" operations, will be examined in this part of the book.

Procurement

Procurement is described at obtaining the right goods at the right place, with the right quality, at the right time, the right price, the right quantity.

Before buying any goods or services, fundamental questions to be asked are:

*   Is it needed?
*   Can the need be met in another way?
*   Is it already to be found elsewhere within the company?
*   Can the requirement be met by sharing rather that purchasing?
*   Can the requirement be met by renting rather than by purchasing?
*   Is the quantity required essential?
*   Can it serve any useful purpose after its initial use?
*   Is the value added to the business, greater than, the total cost of ownership?

The Total cost of ownership (TCO)

This is a philosophy that includes Value. The Total Cost of Ownership sees that the benefit of ownership only comes when the value added to the business through owning the asset, is greater than, the TCO.

Conceptually therefore:

TCO = Price +total acquisition cost (TAC) +Life cycle costs (LCC) or whole life costs (WLC).

Both TAC and WLC are examined below:

Total Acquisition Cost
This is the Price Paid plus, all the "other" costs paid by the buyer:
- Quality e.g. errors, defects, returns
- Delivery e.g. modes, time scales
- Delivery Performance e.g. non availability, unreliability
- Lead Time e.g. stock financing
- Packing e.g. point of display repacks
- Warehousing e.g. extra handling
- Inventory e.g. product deterioration
- New Supplier e.g. start-ups, assessments, negotiations
- Administration e.g. orders processing

The "real" question to ask is what are these "other" costs?

Whole life costing (WLC)
This is the same as Life Cycle costing and can be defined as: "The systematic consideration of all relevant costs and revenues associated with the acquisition and ownership of the asset and a means of comparing options and their associated cost and revenue over a period of time."

WLC covers:
- Initial capital/procurement costs, e.g. design, construction, installation, purchase, or leasing fees and charges
- Future costs, e.g. all operating costs (rent, rates, cleaning, inspection, maintenance, repair, placements/renewals, energy, dismantling, disposal, security, and management). Unplanned and unexpected maintenance/refurbishment may amount to more than half of the initial capital spent
- Opportunity costs, e.g. the cost of not having the money available for alternative investments, which would earn money, or the interest payable on loans to finance work

Procurement portfolios

These show the critical aspects to be examined to establish the strategic importance of a product to the business.

Kraljic's Risk/Spend by products and by relationships
Product categories:

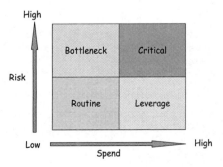

These indicate that different products have different strategic requirements to a business:

- Routine items: Routine buying of commodities from a well-developed supplier marketplace
- Critical items: The need here is to ensure the supply and reduce the risk of non supply; constant availability is key here
- Leverage items: here a high volume is purchased from a market with many competing suppliers, therefore obtaining the lowest cost is relatively easy
- Bottleneck items: These are difficult to source, for example suppliers of "unique items"

World class purchasing guidelines:

- What are the annual spend and requirements of the purchasing portfolios?
- Is there a programme to reduce the procurement lead times?
- Is component variety limited by looking closely at users specifications (avoiding brand names), and duplicated purchasing
- What are the supplier assessment methods and supplier management policies?
- Do all communication processes deliver understanding?
- What codification is used?
- Is supply chain management used?
- Is end to end product evaluation used by applying the total costs of ownership (TCO)?
- What programme is there to develop relationships with users/customers and with external suppliers
- Is there a culture of Total Quality?
- Have buyers changed from being reactive order placers to be proactive commodity managers?
- Should you outsource or manage procurement yourself?
- Is there a programme to reduce the supplier base to a small number of qualified suppliers fully integrated into the business?
- Is there a culture of continuous improvement?

The following case study looks at procurement in NHS Supplies:

This describes the situation seen by its author back in the late 1990s, and does illustrate the needed central role of supply chain management in procurement.

Case Study: NHS Supplies

The traditional trading patterns of the past decades are changing rapidly in almost every sector and the NHS is no exception. The main drivers for this change are technological developments, an expanding trade and a dramatic increase in customer expectations. In order to exploit these opportunities, supply chain management, and purchasing in particular, is being put under the spotlight. In my experience as a consultant, standards of purchasing vary tremendously within the NHS. There are some excellent departments with high-calibre individuals who are imaginative and skilled in a wide range of modern purchasing techniques. But there are also some buyers, who are less imaginative, having lower skill levels and are often more interested in filing than doing a good deal.

In one trust I examined recently, a 17-strong department was responsible for using just 40 per cent or so of its £60 million total spend. All of the expenditure on pharmaceuticals, and most of that on the estate, was outside the involvement of the department. Even in areas where purchasing was involved, such as IT consumables and food, the rest of the organisation's view of purchasing staff was that "their job is to order what we tell them to".

Some problems were evident: there were too many petty controls, for example, far too much emphasis on paper pushing and very little real added value.

There was also a severe lack of useful information with which to make sensible decisions. For example, if a buyer wanted to know how much was spent with a particular supplier in the previous year, what else was bought from them, how they had been performing recently or how their prices had moved, it was difficult and time consuming to access the data.

If they wanted to ask more fundamental questions, such as by how much a supplier's performance was improving or declining, whether any of its main competitors were also supplying the trust, or how many different users in the trust had dealt with that supplier, it was virtually impossible to find the answers. Yet, access to information like this is the first step in a purchasing improvement programme.

One reason for the problems was the culture of suspicion and blame in which the function operated. And this kind of stultifying environment brings its own problems. Good staffs with imagination and intelligence either leave through frustration, or gradually become disenchanted. In some organisations, keeping your head down and blaming others when something goes wrong is the only way to survive.

What trusts like this need is a three-fold programme. First they must change the structure of the purchasing department, promote the best staff and encourage new employees to adopt modern ideas and gain experience of up-to-date buying techniques. Second, they must improve their purchasing systems, so that administration is more streamlined and information is more accessible.

Third, and perhaps most importantly, they must embark on a scheme of attitude and culture change, so that everyone with supplier contact - not just those in purchasing -understands the main implications of their behaviour and how their actions affect the way their suppliers respond and behave towards them. These staff needs to be given new ideas and the enthusiasm to act on them. If they can grasp the nettle and make these changes, then really dramatic improvements should be forthcoming.

Ineffective departments add cost, not value. They miss the chance to save money by not taking a more commercial approach to agreeing and awarding contracts. They miss opportunities to encourage suppliers to improve their quality of service, product, and delivery. They also miss opportunities to drive down internal costs through efficient processing, and to drive down external costs through managing and removing the "extras", which so often creep in and can sometimes add as much as 25 per cent to a price.

Besides this, service levels can be substandard. While there could be a high level of stock available, for example, it could take up to seven days to get that stock to the ward, or office, that needs it. World-class organisations get stock items delivered in minutes, rather than days. Taking a professional approach to purchasing is crucial. Not only does it add value - through the achievement of bought-in cost savings, better supplier relationships and quality improvements - it also helps organisations to minimise most of the commercial and legal risks that can accompany the sourcing process. It is vital that NHS trusts' purchasing staff are well resourced, trained, and supported. There must be the procedural arid organisational backing in place to allow departments to operate effectively and really add value.

One technique that is currently being adopted in many industries is supply chain integration. True integration provides the ability to balance long-term future capacity and forecasted demand throughout the supply chain. It also helps to identify potential bottlenecks arid constraints, and to find solutions with partners. If applied throughout a trust, it would offer substantial benefits. It would mean that all processes were properly aligned, operating relationships were streamlined, and trouble free and key suppliers were seen as part of the overall process of service delivery. Supply Chain Integration is an emerging and powerful method of purchasing that uses e-commerce and a range of other management tools to integrate and streamline the whole supply chain to produce significant, sustained advantage. It has recently been described as "an alignment of the end-to-end supply chain and the creation of an integrated and high-performance entity that will deliver superior end-customer value".

Examples of organisations exploiting SCI in the consumer electronics and automotive industries show leading firms offering customised products, while achieving significant savings and efficiencies. This involves breaking down barriers and building trust and collaborative relationships with users and suppliers. It is clear that purchasing in the NHS is under scrutiny and unlikely to remain unchanged. The new Purchasing and Supply Agency has a mission to save money and make buying in the NHS more efficient. The changing market place and the demands facing the health service will force a re-evaluation of the whole supply chain. Only by integrating the supply chain can the full benefits be realised. I only hope that purchasers grasp these with both hands.

Source: Supply Management 15 June 2000.

Production

Production and manufacturing in the UK has been relatively late in changing to embrace demand driven needs for smaller, make to order batches. The conflicts between volume and variety are a main aspect in production and traditionally, high volume with low variety (and low price), were seen as the "only way".

However in recent times, changes have been made in those industries that have remained in the UK. For example, the food/drink and car assembly industries have become much more demand driven and this has been reflected back into changing the production methods. Meanwhile, off-shoring has been used for much of the former UK manufacturing and production base, this usually requiring good freight management for the longer transit times; a subject covered in "Logistics Freight Transport-Domestic and International" Emmett (2006). In turn this means that an effective overall supply chain management process is required.

Production Options: Making to Order or Making to Stock.
There is a separation point between forecasting and ordering, as shown by the following diagram, which gives five "positions" or "decoupling points".

The 1-5 positions are separated by Forecasts and Order activities, as below:

1) Make and deliver from stock (MDTS) = Forecast driven
Examples are fast moving food products that are held in regional distribution centres, near to retail outlets

2) Make to stock (MTS) = Forecast driven
Examples are slower moving consumer and food items that are held more centrally in Central Distribution centres

3) Assemble to order (ATO) = Order driven
Furniture and beds are examples of this method of production.

4) Make to order (MTO) = Order driven
Examples here are some PCs and top of the range cars like a Rolls Royce

5) Purchase and make to order (PMTO) = Order driven
High tech and large capital "one off" items are examples here

From a production aspect, the following can be typically found:
1) MDTS: Continuous flow production with very high volume produced but with no product variation; such as with petrol and steel. Such items are known as "runners".

2) MTS: Dedicated line flow production with very high volumes made and with little product variation; the mass production of cars was traditionally a good example.

3) ATO: Mixed product line flow with medium volumes produced of medium product variations; the manufacturing of clothes is an example here as is the "newer" method now used for car assembly. Such items are known as "repeaters"

4) MTO: Batch flow production with lower volumes of high product variation; job shops like printers being an example here.

5) PMTO: Job shop production of very low volumes but very high product variations; project one off items like ships being one example. Such items may be called "strangers" as they are not found too often!

These positions give rise to the following supply chain basic options where:

- "Push" involves forecast driven activity that pushes and supplies stock towards the customer, where it is held to await the customers demand orders. It involves the inventory holding of finished goods and is "risky" in as much as it dealing more with uncertainty in demand.
- "Pull" involves actual demand orders pulling stock through the supply chain from the point of supply. It is responsive directly to these orders and involves the products matching exactly what customers order. It involves the holding stock of semi finished work in progress, or even no inventory at all (as with DP5), where raw materials are ordered to specifically manufacture a customer order. There is less risk with this option as nothing is more certain than the customers order.

A comparison of the DP1-5 options follows (overleaf):

Activity	MTS(1/2) "Make then sell" Forecast "Push" Supply-demand	MTO(4/5) "Sell then make" Order "Pull" Demand-supply
Main driver	Forecasts. Structured planning and scheduling.	Orders. Sense and respond using real time information.
Buying	Is for anticipated needs by instructing suppliers. Focus on cost and quality.	Is for daily needs using involved suppliers. Focus on speed, quality and flexibility.
Product	Standardised products. Cost driven.	Can be bespoke and modular. More quality driven.
Customer lead time	Fast and short	Slower
Production	Low cost as uses long production run lengths. High average utilisation.	Higher costs and short run lengths and fast production line changes. Excess buffer capacity is used
Inventory	Cost is in finished goods and uses safety stock. Stock is viewed as an asset and as a protection	Cost is in raw materials and work in progress with little safety stock. Stock is viewed as a liability
Distribution	Storage costs are high with low transport costs (as moving in bulk).	Storage costs are low with transport costs being higher as moving smaller quantities more frequently

The "make then sell" position is well represented by the historic Henry Ford expression of "you can have colour you want, as long it as it is black" and also from the traditional manufacture/assembly of consumer goods.

Nowadays, cars for example, follow the "assemble to order" (position three) that involves assembling a specific order from stocks of components/work in progress. This method of production represents for many, the optimum production trade-off in the supply chain, as final assembly is only taking place on receipt of the order; the final product production being "postponed" until a firm order is received. It will also mean of course, adopting a more challenging form of supply chain management.

World class production guidelines:
* Is product delivered on time in full (OTIF) more than 99% of the time
* Is there a programme to reduce production lead times?
* Is material received fit for purpose and supplied to the point of use without inspection?
* Do all communication processes deliver understanding?
* Does the layout enable sequential operations?
* Are set up times reduced to the minimum?
* Is supply chain management used?
* Are non value added costs progressively reduced?
* Is there a culture of Total Quality?

- Is there an active policy to keep areas clean and tidy?
- Does the product design facilitate production?
- Is there a culture of continuous improvement?
- Should you outsource or manage production yourself?

Meanwhile, the following case study shows the view of one organisations production within supply chain management.

Case Study: Lessons from Dell

One company that is building on a history of excellent supply-chain management to meet the Internet challenge is Dell Computer Corporation. Dell uses supply chain management to implement and continuously improve its "direct" model. This model continues to be a major differentiation for Dell in the ultra-competitive PC market.

The Dell "direct" model demonstrates the value and effectiveness of supply-chain integration:

- Dell buys components just in time, benefiting from the latest (i.e., the lower component) prices.
- For Dell, "build-to-order" means exactly that: No resources are committed until a customer order is received.

Through combining these and other supply chain management practices, Dell is able to offer:

- A wide product range
- Competitive prices
- Short delivery lead times, without sacrificing margins and with minimum inventory

Dell continues to develop and improve capabilities of its supply chain. For example, by the end of 1998 the Dell web site was generating revenue of over $14 million a day, an increase from around $2 million at the end of 1997. The web site makes online ordering quick and convenient by allowing customers to specify the product features they want, and by instantly giving them a price quote.

To further differentiate itself in the corporate market, Dell has created "Premier Pages." These are web sites dedicated to corporate clients that can be accessed by a client's authorised employees to research, configure, and price PCs before they buy. Each web site holds client-specific information, such as preferred configurations and pricing. This information improves order accuracy and simplifies Dell's order entry processes. For customers, the cost of buying PCs is greatly reduced.

Source: Managing your supply chain in the 21st century, PRT&Mc

Physical distribution

Definitions can be important to clarify thought and are especially so, when one person understands a term to mean one thing, but then another person understands the same term differently.

This has been especially happening for example, in the UK from the mid 1990s with "Logistics". Logistics, which originally encompassed the whole supply chain, is now, being referred to by many companies as a new name for transport, or for warehousing/stores or for distribution. Third party transport companies are also now beginning to call themselves supply chain management companies. In the UK, one can observe the new name on a freight transport vehicle that before was called "Fred Smith Transport," is now called "Fred Smith Logistics". Logistics can therefore be a confusing word. Additionally, some people use the term logistics to describe their own internal company process, and use the supply chain term, when they are dealing with external suppliers/customers. At the risk of further confusion, others also call their internal logistics processes, the internal supply chain!

Physical Distribution meanwhile is about delivering the right goods to the right place at the right time and at the right cost. This "rights of distribution" definition represents in a simple way, the objectives for distribution. Distribution therefore involves the combining of transport with warehousing, and is a term that is often applied to mainly finished goods. However, it may also by used by suppliers who are delivering product to their customer, perhaps of raw materials and semi-finished work-in -progress goods. Suppliers are also concerned with getting the "rights" correct and as far as that supplier is concerned, the raw materials can be for them, the finished goods.

Meanwhile, when readers hear the three terms of logistics, supply chain and distribution, they are strongly recommended to ensure they have the full understanding of what the originator means by the specific word. This can be very important and prevent confusions; for example, "Fred Smith Logistics" is unlikely to have a clue about whether to outsource the manufacture of sub assemblies or whether these can be manufactured internally. This would often be strategic supply chain decision (but then again, some would say it is a strategic logistics decision).

Distribution and the Supply chain

Physical Distribution is the method by which goods move from one location to another. It is an essential function in product supply chains as it provides for the physical movement between the suppliers and customers. This movement can be for raw materials, sub assemblies/ work in progress, or for the finished goods; it can take place over shorter distances on a national basis, or the movement can be over longer distances and on a global basis. In demand driven supply chains, warehouses are mainly used for storing goods, or involve more sorting activities; both being required to largely feed external customers. In the supply driven supply chains, then warehouses often are re-named as stores, and are holding stocks to feed internal activities, like production.

Distribution and the Economy

In the UK and Europe, there is a close relationship between freight movement and economic growth measured by gross domestic product (GDP). This is because freight transport, and especially road haulage as the dominant mode, has important and wide-ranging effects on UK supply chain management. Road is dominant simply because of the other modes, and particularly rail transport, are currently imperfect substitutes; in particular:
*   Rail transportation and inland waterway transportation are not able to offer the same quality (in terms of cost, speed, flexibility, availability and reliability) as road transportation
*   The capacity of rail transportation is not sufficient to guarantee a reliable transportation for the majority of goods currently being transported by road

The nature of the distribution service demanded will depend to some extent on the nature of the materials transported. The important elements here are as follows:
*   nature of product
*   value density
*   perishable nature (physically and economically)
*   hazardous physical characteristics (size, liquid/gas)

The structural characteristics of the supply chain systems, which are of most significance in determining the sensitivity of the transport system, are as follows:
*   number and location of facilities; including production plants, warehouses and transfer facilities
*   the transportation modes currently used
*   number and location of the suppliers
*   size and location of inventories
*   number and location of the customers
*   information systems employed

Transport and warehouses are both therefore, integral parts of the supply/demand chain/ pipeline infrastructure and are examined more fully in *"Logistics Freight Transport - Domestic and International"* (Emmett 2005) and *"Excellence in Warehouse Management"* (Emmett 2006).

World class distribution guidelines
The following are the basic points that everyone involved in managing distribution must be alert to:
*   Do you need each warehouse in the distribution network?
*   Is there a programme to reduce all the distribution lead times?
*   How can each item be packed?
*   What products should be kept and where?
*   Is product delivered on time in full (OTIF) more than 95% of the time
*   Is supply chain management used?
*   How many times are products handled?
*   Are products stored in relation to the flow/rate of movement?
*   Is the warehouse layout and transport network optimal?

- Is the right transport mode being used?
- What are the operational standards?
- Do we have a multi-skilled work force?
- Is there a culture of continuous improvement?
- Should we outsource or manage distribution ourselves?
- Is there a culture of total quality?

Meanwhile the following case study illustrates one companies view on distribution in supply chain management:

Case Study: Dunlop & Goodyear UK tyre distribution

The formation of a global joint venture between tyre manufacturers Goodyear and Dunlop in 1999 has had huge implications for the UK supply chain and has brought significant opportunities to improve performance.

Since it came into being the joint venture has merged deliveries of its different brands to retailers, opened a national distribution centre, rationalised its network of depots, and replaced its fleet through logistics partner Christian Salvesen.

The Logistics Development Manager of Goodyear Dunlop says the aim has been to capitalise on synergies of the joint venture and to improve customer service. "The key elements in our operation are accuracy of deliveries, providing a next-day service to retailers, giving customers the ability to get hold of information and, obviously, controlling costs," he says.

Goodyear Dunlop accounts for around 25-40% of the tyre replacement market in the UK, dependent on the market segment, and sells in excess of seven million tyres to its customers, who include retailers, car manufacturers, small garages and wholesalers. That is around six or seven different supply chains to deal with.

When the joint venture was formed, the first task was to combine deliveries of the various brands to customers. This was a complex challenge as a network of outbases around the country was used to cross-dock product and divide it up for delivery to customers. When the two companies came together, seven different warehouses fed this network.

Once combined deliveries had been achieved, a more fundamental restructuring of the logistics network was undertaken. The most important element of this was a new national distribution centre capable of loading delivery vehicles in drop order so that the products would not have to be handled again at outbases.

Tyres are now loaded in 5m boxes, which are trunked by third party contractor, Christian Salvesen and then swapped onto delivery vehicles - without the contents being touched - at Salvesen multi--user depots which have replaced the outbases. The move to the new network is already largely in place and will be completed by the end of November. Salvesen multi--user sites at Bovey Tracey in Devon, Bracknell, Bury St Edmunds, Darlington, Gloucester, Leigh, Motherwell and Rochester are being used for the operation.

The 46,000sq m national distribution centre, known as Tyrefort, is at Fort Dunlop in Birmingham and was developed by a distribution property specialist under a sale and leaseback deal on land previously owned by Dunlop until the joint venture was formed with Goodyear in 1999. The facility, which also includes a 4,600sq m UK head office for Goodyear Dunlop, has 47 loading doors, yard capacity for 70 vehicles, and 13m clear headroom.

The first depot to be replaced was Hamm's-Hall only a few miles away from Tyrefort in July and the NDC operation has gradually been built up since that time. They considered several scenarios with the network
including having two regional distribution centres - Manchester to cover the north and London to cover the south - but upon examination this option was found to be more expensive than operating from a single facility.

The centre has the capacity to store over 1 million tyres and is capable of a throughput of more than 80,000 tyres a day. There are several different types of racking used to accommodate the different products which, taking into account the different types and sizes, number 1,500. There are separate areas for fast-moving and slow-moving lines.

The put-away of tyres into storage is undertaken by Goodyear Dunlop operatives, who also carry out the picking function. Once the tyres reach the loading bay Christian Salvesen, takes over responsibility for them until they are delivered to the customer.

Use of IT systems is crucial in managing the flow of tyres. Orders for next-day delivery are taken until 1730 hours on Goodyear Dunlop's SAP system and are then transferred into Christian Salvesen's automatic routing software, supplied by Paragon. Proposed routes are then fed into Salvesen's bespoke system, which sequences deliveries and is capable of making delivery information available to customers over the Internet.

The routing information is then fed back into Goodyear Dunlop's IT systems, which use it to form picking lists and monitor their progress - if picking of an order gets behind, the system alerts warehouse staff so that more people can be allocated to keeping the order on track. When the tyres arrive at the loading bay, they are checked against the original order by Salvesen staff before being put onto the vehicle.

Goodyear Dunlop and Christian Salvesen staff works as closely together as possible. A joint uniform has been created and drivers are given product knowledge training about the tyres.

Once the deliveries have been made to the customers the vehicles are given a route back, so that they can pick up anything that needs to be returned to Tyrefort. All the time they are on the road their movements are tracked using satellite technology, this enables the traffic office to know exactly where they are and to warn them about serious congestion.

Goodyear Dunlop's decision to appoint Christian Salvesen as its logistics contractor came after an extensive tendering process. Previously Dunlop had used Christian Salvesen and Exel while Goodyear had used Exel and Lex. The joint venture wanted a partner, which could help streamline the network, provide the right amount of IT infrastructure and create the right relationship with its customers.

The contract has a reward mechanism built into it to give incentives to Salvesen to make the operation, which aims to maintain accuracy levels of 99.6%, as efficient as possible. This is calculated using a series of key performance indicators covering customer service, financial performance, people, and operational costs.

In order to improve the operation and make sure it is running as it should there are weekly, monthly and quarterly meetings. Salvesen is given information about the joint venture's future needs and is kept informed about where the business is going.

Extracts from source: "Getting to Grips", Motor Transport 31 October 2002.

Marketing

It is customer demand that drives the "total" supply chain; therefore the marketing process has some useful viewpoints. As has been usefully noted by Peter Drucker:

"Marketing is so basic that it cannot be considered a separate function. It is the whole business seen from the point of view of its final result, that is, for the customers' point of view. Business success is not determined by the producer but by the customer."

It is interesting to observe that marketing, like supply chain management, has gone thorough many changes in recent years:

Forward marketing "Old"	Reverse Marketing "New"
Production led as everyone would buy	Market led to determine what everyone needs to buy
Design and make the product first	Find out the customer needs and then design the product
High volume, low variety = "Any colour you want as long as it is black." (Henry Ford)	Customers needs are known in advance of production
Sell what produce and promote unsought goods	Make only what can sell and make to order
Focus on sellers needs and make to stock	Customer satisfaction and loyalty

Basic tenets of marketing are as follows and it will be observed that these tenets are the same for demand-led supply chain management:
- Customers are the basis of the business
- We need to know who they are and what they need
- We must anticipate customers changing needs
- Everyone in the organisation is involved in marketing
- We must develop long term relationships with our customers

The Marketing "Ps"

A cornerstone of a marketing approach is the six "Ps":

Product/service supplied looks at the following:
- Features (Physical, service, psychological)
- What does it "look like"?
- What will be delivered?
- Description, including benefits
- Value to the customer/WIIFM (what is in it for me)?
- Customisation/tailoring?

Place
- Distribution channels; how to get products to the marketplace e.g. direct, via wholesalers, via retailers etc.
- Market positioning and competition in the marketplace
- Inventory levels; where and what format to hold?
- Physical distribution management; the moving of products to the marketplace
- Internet marketing and "e" shopping

Physical facilities
- Premises
- Impacts to first time visitor/users
- Stationery/PR Material/appearance

Price
- Cost plus process , or
- Market nature/market based prices?
- Competition pricing
- Customer perceptions and expectations

Promotion
- Communications
- Two way/Understanding
- "The object of communication is to prevent misunderstanding"
- "The meaning of communication is in its effect"
- Moving through stages of unaware-aware-comprehension-conviction-action
- Using negotiation/persuasion

People
- Image
- Skills and experiences
- Attitude and behaviour

Working through the "Ps" will show the basis of customer's needs and the resultant differentiation required and supply chain design.

World class marketing guidelines
- Who are the key customers?
- What differentiates the company from the competition?
- When was the last SWOT (Strengths/Weaknesses, Opportunities/Threats) analysis undertaken?
- When was the last PEST (Political, Economic, Social, and Technological) analysis undertaken?
- Is the market place fully understood?
- Is there a culture of Total Quality? (Quality is examined later in the section: Supply Chain Alternative Approaches)
- What us the market segmentation policy?
- Do customer contact staff have the authority to fully resolve problems
- Do all communication processes deliver understanding?
- Is the "time to market" at a minimum
- Is there a flexible workforce?
- Is there a culture of continuous improvement?
- Is the company a market driven one?
- Is supply chain management used?

Supply chain performance and Key Performance Indicators (KPIs)

The basis and origin of these will be from the following:
- Historic data, for example comparison of actual performance against the expected plan; financial budgets (see below) are one way and a common tool to do this
- Internal comparison with other operations and sites within an organisation
- External benchmarking with other organisations

One of the main performance measures, used in market capitalism by organisations are financial measures, as these are commonly understood and are seen to be objective. The core control mechanism that is used here is financial budgets. A budget is a plan and a forecast in financial terms, covering a specified period of time.

Budgetary control involves the setting of objectives, in monetary terms, and enables managers to plan and control the resources they are responsible for. When regular comparisons are made between what was planned and what actually occurred, any variances can be remedied or the plans can be revised.

Effective Budgeting

An organisations finance people are likely to have overall control. Indeed, in some companies they may be totally responsible for setting budgets and communicating them to the relevant personnel who have responsibility for managing them. In other companies, budgets are set by individual department or section managers. Such an approach can motivate some managers by involving them in the activity, giving them ownership and responsibility for their budgets.

There is no perfect budgetary control system. If it is to be effective, though, it should be tailored as closely as possible to the needs of the company. An effective budgetary system will be possible if the following points are adhered to:
- There must be a system in place for the efficient collection and processing of accounting data
- All of the management team must be committed to and involved in the budgetary process
- The will to act on budgetary information quickly and positively, must be encouraged
- Managers must be trained in budgetary control and interpretation techniques
- Good lines of communication must exist within the organisation

The following process can be used to construct a budget:
- Determine the assumptions, for example, the sales forecasts, the future unit cost estimations etc.
- Specify the demand
- Analyse the process and resources needed
- Apply the financial factors, for example in warehouse picking, 50 labour hours at a labour cost of £"x" per hour, gives the labour cost per day for picking
- Evaluate; to see if the plan looks realistic and in conformity with expectations from others in the organisation. This may mean iteration is then required
- Finalise the forecast plan

The use of budgetary control systems has the following advantages as follows:
- Resources are controlled efficiently
- Motivation of those involved can increase if they are included in the budgeting process
- Decisions can be based on the examination of problems and corrective action
- Plans can be reviewed regularly
- The activities of the various functions, in the company, can be coordinated effectively

Budget control is not without critics as the following shows:
- Budget setting and monitoring are time consuming and can prevent people performing their jobs
- As mentioned above, planning is an inexact science and the results can be totally different from what was anticipated
- Some managers may be happy to achieve only the budget targets and not push beyond this
- The setting of budgets can de-motivate, if targets are imposed or set at levels that are felt to be unrealistic

Some financial budgets can therefore actually constrain managers and prevent them from taking opportunities which may arise.

Financial performance in the supply chain

As seen earlier, supply chain management there can be are some inherent problems with using traditional financial measures, for example with linking the financial "outcome" to:
- the input operational efficiencies
- the level of service delivered

Whilst we examined finance impacts in the supply chain earlier in part 2.0, Supply Chain Management contributes and supplements financial performance, for example:
- gives us focus on where assets are deployed and how these can be "sweated" or used more productively, for example increasing volume throughout with fixed cost assets
- turning over stock quicker to improve cash flow and reduce stock holding costs
- freeing up capital invested in fixed assets, for example by outsourcing
- integrating with external players to reduce exposure and foster concentration on "core" competencies

When relating the earlier examined Theory of Constraints (TOC) to the normal financial performance measures of companies (nett profit, return on investment and cash flow), Goldratt notes that these are all actually affected by the following operational measures:
- Increases in throughput (in TOC, Throughput is the rate at which money is generated by sales)
- Reducing inventory (Inventory is money invested, awaiting sale)
- Reducing costs/operating expenses (money spent turning inventory into throughput)

This view in TOC is therefore very supportive of the importance of the supply chain operational aspects and of all the associated flows/throughputs; in addition to the inventory holdings and the costs. Finally, the following aspects have been noted, for obtaining profitable performance for a supply chain (based on *"How to survive in a volatile world"* in Logistics Europe June 2002).

1) Product and service portfolio management
- Detect product life cycles shifts and modify underlying models
- Customer segmentation allows targeted service offerings that increase margins
- New products can capture the market potential more directly

2) Working capital efficiency
- Reduce inventory and payment cycles
- Rapid flows without disruptive risk

3) Cost to serve
- Cost management is reported by product and by channel.
- Checking the planned to actual profitability of each customer order
- Use of TCO/TAC models

4) Asset efficiency
- Utilisation of assets goes straight to the bottom line
- Outsourcing will reduce working capital
- Whoever owns the assets has the direct bottom line impact
- Tax efficiency
- Contribute to maintain operational competitiveness whilst minimising global tax rate

Supply chain performance drivers

Supply chain performance will therefore be driven by all of the following aspects:
- Organisational configuration of the physical assets and product/information flows, (for example: elimination of inventory whilst optimally balancing costs, service levels and availability)
- Management of the supply chain (for example, flexibility and a reliance on quality)
- External relationships with suppliers and customers (for example: a share to gain approach)
- Internal structures and management of the supply chain (for example: elimination of all barriers to all the internal and external activities)
- Information systems (for example: transparent flows of goods/information)

Activity Based Costing (ABC)

As has been seen earlier, the Theory of Constraints (TOC) sees a different world in viewing what causes what and what is the relative importance. Costs (and the TOC view of the "Cost World"), are only one source to use in control and in making improvements. Whilst we shall be returning more fully to improvements in Section 5.0; we shall now look at the use of Activity Based Costing (ABC) in Goldratts TOC "Cost World". Activity Based Costing has brought a "new" focus on costing with the premise that costs do not just happen; as, activities use resources and using resources give rise to costs; therefore knowledge of the resource use is needed to understand the costs. The traditional view of cost control and (the accounting terminology used) is one that looks at:
- Where costs were incurred (cost centre)
- What the cost was (account)
- When it occurred (period)
- Who was responsible (budget holder)

But, here the following two key words are missing:
- Why we spent the money?
- How are we going to reduce it, or how to get more value from, it?

It is the activities/processes, which lead to the resource use, which then give rise to costs. Therefore, to control costs you have to control the resource and also, to manage the process.

In controlling costs, there is the need to control and/or reduce the resources represented by those costs.

Additionally, costs will also result from "Waste" in the resources; the resources being:
*   Labour
*   Machinery
*   Materials
*   Money
*   Minutes
*   Information

Examples of such waste and losses in resources, are as follows:
*   Machinery/equipment downtime e.g. unexpected breakdowns, set up times and adjustments, low utilisation etc.
*   Minutes/time/speed losses e.g. idling and stoppages, reduced speeds, slow lead times etc.
*   Materials/quality losses e.g. process defects, scrap and rework rejects/returns etc.

For a business to increase profits in the long term, then the following "standard" and normal cost options are available:
*   Reduce the usage of resources/costs whilst maintaining sales
*   Pay less per unit of cost resource whilst still buying the same resource and maintaining sales
*   Eliminate unprofitable activities (or in-activities)
*   Increase sales (but competition may quickly catch up/take these sales away)

The relationship here to "standard" cost descriptors are as follows:
*   Fixed costs: Do not change and do not vary directly, in relation to the activity/throughput
*   Variable costs: Do change and vary in relation to the activity/throughput
*   Total costs: Are the fixed and variable costs added together for a given level of activity/throughput

As was seen earlier, the control of costs is often undertaken through budgets. With traditional cost budget control, activity based costing sees the following disadvantages:
*   Focus is on the comparison to the budget and that this can be an industry in itself with "ritual" bargaining, accompanied with finding sophisticated ways of breaking the rules
*   No indication of year to year performance
*   No indication of cost and process and throughput dynamics
*   Silo cost centre mentality encouraging parochial, sub-optimisation
*   No focus on process efficiencies
*   Are reactive "damage reports"

Alternative controls from ABC are available however, as follows:
*   Reporting the resource usage/throughputs/inventories
*   Activity/process KPIs
*   Comparisons to past year data
*   Costs are compared cumulatively with trends
*   Emphasis is placed on pro-active continuous improvements, rather than "beat the budget" or finding "sophisticated reasons for failure"

With activity based costing, the view taken, is that to control costs, then, the following needs to be undertaken:
* Look at the underlying resource
* Work out what the KPI is for that resource
* Control through that KPI

Activity based costing (ABC) represents a useful alternative to cost control and to productivity and to improvement. It also fits neatly with the earlier described Theory of Constraints views on the "Cost World".

Supply chain performance and measurement

The entire supply chain performance can be controlled and monitored by the following measurement tools:

Description	Measurement tool	Definition	Units
Customer orders fulfilment	On time/in Full rate (OTIF).	% orders OTIF	%
	Lead time.	Receipt of order to despatched/delivered	Hours/Days
Customer satisfaction	Customer Survey	A sampling survey to ask for customers experiences, for example: -Support available -Product availability -Flexibility -Reliability -Consistency -Comparison to the competition	% satisfied
Supply management	On time/in full (OTIF).	As above	%
	Supplier Survey.	As above customer survey	% satisfied
	Effectiveness.	Year over year improvements	%
	Lead Time	Time placed order- time available for use	Hours/Days
Inventory (measure for each holding place of raw materials, work in progress and finished goods)	Forecast accuracy.	Actual/Forecast sales per SKU.	%
	Availability.	Ordered / Delivered Per SKU.	%
	On hand.	Value on hand/daily delivered value.	Days

Cash flow	Cash to cash.	Time from paying suppliers, to time paid by customers	Days
Quality	Quality.	Non conformances, as appropriate	Per 100 or 1000 or million
Operations	Utilisations.	Used/Available.	} Units } Hours } Costs
	Productivity.	Actual/Standard.	
	Costs.	Actual/Standard.	
	Lead times.	Time start/time completed per operation, (see the earlier Lead time section).	Hours or Days
People Relationships	Internal.	Absence rates Staff turnover rates	% %
	Internal	Opinion surveys, for example: - Support given - Development - Morale - Work conditions - Communication - etc	% satisfied
	External.	Sampling Survey, as used in the above customer surveys	% satisfied
Costs	Total supply chain or per operation cost.	Cost per time period/ Units.	£ per unit

Benchmarking

Benchmarking is the process of continually measuring and comparing a business's processes against comparable processes, so that a business can be improved. The key components involved are as follows::

- Plan what has to be benchmarked, set up a team, document the current process and establish performance measures
- Search for a partner/identify the best performers (by direct approaches, benchmarking clubs, databases etc.)
- Conduct site visits to the best companies
- Observe and gather data using detailed surveys of their methods and processes
- Analyse the data to identify performance gaps
- Adapt/change to improve performance

Benchmarking therefore looks for "Best Practice":

- internally
- with competitive companies
- within similar functions in "any" company
- outside of the industry

Meanwhile, the "Best Practice Company Characteristics" for benchmarking, has been defined by the DTI as follows:

1) Appreciate and develop employees potential by:
- creating a culture of empowerment and customer focus
- invest in people through good communications and personal development
- flatten the organisational structure

2) They know their customers and:
- continually learn from them
- appreciate customer demands are a springboard for innovation and greater competitiveness

3) Constantly introduce new products and services:
- through being knowledgeable about competitors
- encouraging and promoting innovation
- focus on core business
- construct strategic alliances where appropriate

Finally, here the results of one benchmarking study are shown in the following case study:

Case Study: Benchmarking: UK Drinks Sector Supply Chains

Companies involved:
- Five soft drinks brand owners
- Four beer and cider brand owners
- Five drinks wholesalers

Huge cost variations were found:
- Transport delivery ranged from £10 to £26 a pallet delivered
- Inventory value as percentage sales 100-300 times

Customer service levels varied:
- Right first time ranged from 93 to 99.7 %

Conclusions:
- Fragmented understanding about supply chain costs
- Unclear service level agreements with suppliers
- Little disciplined customer ordering
- Need to look at whole supply chain

Source: Benchmarking Study reported in IFW 27 November 2000

Contingency planning

Contingency planning is the process by which plans are put in place to ensure that all operations and services can recover and continue should a serious incident occur. It is not just about reactive measures, but will also focus on proactive measures of reducing the risk of a disaster in the first instance.

It is vital that any organisation takes seriously the development and maintenance of the disaster recovery or business continuity plan. It is not one of those tasks that can be left until someone has time to deal with it. A serious incident can affect the organisation at any time and disruptions to operations can be a serious matter; for example, if one of your operations was to stop operating right now, how would you do, for example, on the following:

- Advising customers
- Ensuring continuity of service (today and thereafter)
- Advising suppliers
- Handling vehicles already scheduled to make deliveries (in and outbound)

A contingency plan therefore needs to be developed by a team representing all functional areas of the organisation. If the organisation is large enough, a formal project needs to be established, which must have approval and support from the top management.

It is a fact, for many organisations that have been involved in a disaster where their contingency plans failed, actually ceased trading within 18 months following the disaster. Contingency planning is therefore important and many organisations will not do business with third party service providers (for example, those in ICT and Distribution), if contingency planning is not practised within the service provider's organisation.

Contingency planning can be regarded as either just the recovery of the infrastructure that delivers a service, such as the warehouse or its WMS; or, the much further reaching process of Business Continuity Planning , which ensures that the whole end-to-end business and supply chain process can continue should a serious incident occur.

Planning: first steps

One of the first contingency planning tasks to be undertaken is to prepare a comprehensive list of the potentially serious incidents that could affect the normal operations of the business. This list should include all possible incidents no matter how remote the likelihood of their occurrence.

Against each item listed a probability rating should be noted. Each incident should also be rated for potential impact severity level. From this information, it will become much easier to frame the plan in the context of the real needs of the organization.
This step therefore prioritises the operations and businesses to be recovered; indeed some refer to it as a Business Impact Analysis and/or Risk Assessment as this step identifies the assets, threats, vulnerabilities and countermeasures.

Developing the plan

Once the assessment stage has been completed, the structure of the plan can be established. The plan will contain a range of milestones to move the organisation from its disrupted status towards a return to normal operations; it evaluates the options for recovery.

The first important milestone is the process which deals with the immediate aftermath of the disaster. This may involve the emergency services or other specialists who are trained to deal with extreme situations.

The next stage is to determine which critical business functions need to be resumed and in what order. The plan will of necessity be detailed, and will identify key individuals who should be familiar with their duties under the plan.

Testing the plan

Once this plan has been developed it must be subjected to rigorous testing. The testing process itself must be properly planned and should be carried out in a suitable environment to reproduce authentic conditions in so far as this is feasible.

The plan must be tested by those persons who would undertake those activities if the situation being tested occurred in reality. The test procedures should be documented and the results recorded. This is important to ensure that feedback is obtained for fine tuning the plan; it is important to audit both the plan itself and the contingency and back up arrangements supporting it.

Personnel training

This stage is dependent upon the development of the plan and the successful testing and audit of the plans activities. It is necessary that all personnel must be made aware of the plan and is aware of its contents and their own related duties and responsibilities.

Again, it is important that all personnel take the disaster recovery planning seriously, even if the events which would trigger the plan seem remote and unlikely. Obtain feedback from staff in order to ensure that responsibilities and duties are understood; particularly those which require close dependency on actions being taken by others.

Maintaining the plan

The plan must always be kept up to date and applicable to current business circumstances. This means that any changes to the business process or changes to the relative importance of each part of the business process must be properly reflected within the plan.

Someone must be assigned responsibility for ensuring that the plan is maintained and updated regularly and should therefore ensure that information concerning changes to the business process is properly communicated.

Any changes or amendments made to the plan must be fully tested. Personnel should also be kept abreast of such changes in so far as they affect their duties and responsibilities.

Supply Chain Risk

As supply chains become more responsive and integrated, any disruptions cause the supply chain to become fragile with no flow and with slow, or at worse, stopped, supply chains. Also where supply chains become more lean and agile and deliver smaller quantities with lower stock holding and an increased product range being supplied, then the demand they are satisfying is more susceptible to breaks in the links.

A chain is a strong as its weakest link and small changes in one part of the supply chain can cause massive changes elsewhere. Uncertainty therefore exists and plans need to be made for this. This means identifying where the weak and the bottleneck/choke parts are in a supply chain and developing contingency plans, for example, alternative methods and back up operations.

The key is to have a full knowledge of the way the supply chain works, how it is managed internally and externally by all players and participants and to have both internal and external contingency plans available.

3.0. Action time: Direct Home Delivery PLC (DHD)

Rapid changes are the two key words in the consumer electrical goods sector. New technology constantly arrives on the market and each new product brings with it a swell in consumer demand; however, as the technology becomes more complex, so too, does fulfilment. In the past, a customer may have visited an electrical retailer to buy a television, struggled back to the car with it to take it home and has to plug it in before sitting down to finally watch it.

Growing market expectancy is about the home delivery of such goods. Will a simple box drop suffice? Probably not, according to fulfilment company DHD, a company that believes delivery should go beyond the front door threshold into installation, return and repair, refurbishment or disposal; in other words, a 'cradle to grave' solution. DHD provides a nationwide fulfilment service for consumer electronic goods to clients including manufacturers, retailers, insurance companies and service providers. Customers include major retailers, major manufacturers and major home shipping/catalogue companies. The Chairman believes that beyond the core fulfilment and repair activities there are opportunities driven by a growth in new digital technologies, legislative and economic pressures.

In the brown goods sector, which forms the majority of DHD's business, larger and more technically demanding products such as wall mounted plasma screens, PCs and home networks are increasingly penetrating the market. Such products require two-man home delivery and installation teams. These technologies will also place new demands

---

on the repair service. DHD also has an increasing requirement for a reverse logistics process to cater for returns management for retailers and manufacturers. According to the Chairman, trends such as these, together with the prohibitive costs of in-house management, are likely to drive the brown goods home delivery sector to consolidate around fewer more specialised providers.

Added to this, is the drive to remove excess cost from the supply chain, where electronic retailers will find it difficult to compete with the supply chains of the giant retailers of this world. They, therefore, require better service and variable costs to compete. Outsourcing fulfilment to a contractor that can manage the process and add value is, believes the Chairman, a means to this end. He points to the example of how DHD has helped a major retailer to market leadership in the widescreen television market.

In DHD's opinion, customers are willing to pay for good service; but, bearing in mind that delivery is only an extension of the sale; the brand extension issues make it important that fulfilment is right. So how does DHD get it right? The heart of the company's fulfilment system is its e-hub, which provides core system interconnectivity and allows the company to present from one or many of these systems to a website customised to a client's request. The e-hub also enables business-to-business integration, allowing DHD services to become available within the client's own systems, using the latest technology. At the company's NDC in the Midlands, DHD can maintain a level of stock for clients to enable order fulfilment. Cross docking for stockless operations is undertaken and orders are managed by a computerised order processing system with customer orders being received at the NDC via telephone, the web or EPOS, depending upon the point of sale. When generating an order, product is dispatched to a local operations centre (LOC), of which there are currently 22 nationwide. Products are delivered from the LOC in 3.5 tonne vehicles, each fitted with a tail lift. Customers are contacted to confirm delivery details and which two-hour time slot they prefer. Deliveries are scheduled on the day before and follow a predetermined route. During the customer deliveries, any necessary collections are made for return to the NDC, the manufacturer or the LOC for repair or refurbishment.

Customer deliveries can involve installations using DHD's two man delivery teams and may involve complex jobs such as hanging plasma screens onto customers' walls, demonstrations and the removal of packaging and old product.

Tasks

1. Comment on the way the operations are organised

2. What should be the key performance indicators?

3. How could DHD benchmark their supply-chain performance against historic data and that of similar organisations?

4. What contingency plans should they have?

4.0. Supply Chain Alternative Approaches

In this section we look at the following:

- Total supply chain approaches
- Distribution supply chain approaches
- Inventory approaches
- Financial approaches
- Lean and agile approaches
- Quality management
- Reverse logistics
- Collaborative supply chains
- Supply chain re-thinking
- Trade-offs
- Information and the supply chain
- Systems implementation
- Supply Chain Trends
- World Class Supply Chains
- The Supply Chain Rules

Introduction

With supply chain management being a dynamic and changing philosophy, then varied approaches develop. Whilst some of these are new innovative approaches; other approaches often take one specific aspect of the supply chain (such as time compression), and then "re-package" it using a "catchy" new name (like Quick Response). This is often then also reduced to a two or three letter abbreviation (like QR/ECR).

Such re-packaging can of course be useful, as people will often better focus and identify with "badges." These provide a clearer identification of the approach needed and therefore give direction. We shall examine many of these approaches here and these will be presented as being approaches that are more specific about the "total" supply chain, distribution specific, inventory specific and financial specific approaches.

It should be appreciated this division is arbitrary and overlap will be found, for example, collaboration will be seen to be a common theme. Collaboration will therefore be looked at later in a "separate" section when we shall also look specifically at other approaches like lean/agile, total quality management (TQM) and reverse logistics.

Total supply chain approaches

Quick Response (QR)

QR was originally developed in USA in the 1980s for the domestic apparel and textile industry. It was "the badge" used to encourage national suppliers to react faster to compete with lower priced international imports. It involves shorter lead times with reduced stock levels and demand lead times, so that a faster response can be made to customers order requirements. It requires, adjustments to the re-order levels and also, closer working between suppliers/customers.

Efficient Consumer Response (ECR)

ECR is another USA acronym originally developed for FMCG grocery products. It uses consumer demand to drive the supply chain to deliver exactly when required. Again it uses collaborative approaches supported by ICT.

Collaborative, planning, forecasting and replenishment (CPFR)

CPFR is a collection of business processes that are better enabled by a jointly agreed information system. It aims to change the relationship between suppliers/customers to create an accurate end consumer driven process and information flow. Suppliers/Customers have a common view of consumer demand; they collaborate and coordinate plans, actions and activities through a jointly owned planning system to ensure product availability. CPFR means that the following has to happen:

*   Develop collaborative agreements (and we shall return soon to the subject of, Collaboration)
*   Create joint business plans
*   Create sales forecasts
*   Identify exceptions to the sales forecasts
*   Resolve these exceptions
*   Create the order forecast
*   Identify exceptions to the order forecast
*   Resolve these exceptions
*   Generate the order

It will be seen that collaboration is used to resolve the exceptions in forecasts. CPFR therefore looks to build business relationships by focusing on jointly managed processes with common communication tools.

In summary, CPFR allows for pre-planning rather than reacting; uses ICT/internet technology to reduce inventory and expense, while, increasing sales and improving customer service. CPFR looks to improve the forward visibility of requirements across the entire supply chain.

Distribution supply chain approaches

Postponement

This represents coordinating and delaying the "buy/make/move" activities so that they take place as close as possible to the "sell" demand. Used especially for high value goods that have a high demand uncertainty, postponement involves for example, assemble to order at distribution centres (or with a partner downstream), who customise the order and are located close to the customer.

Consolidation

This is used by many different players in the supply chain who look to benefit from economies in scale, especially of transport, for example:
*   Retailers have primary consolidation centres (PCCs) located in regions near to suppliers where stock is held pending being "called forward." It is then consolidated with other supplier's goods at the PCC into a full load delivered to each of the retailers, nationally located, regional distribution centres (RDCs). From the RDCs, where products are placed into stock or more often, immediately cross-docked on receipt for final delivery to the retailers individual stores.
*   Suppliers have national distribution centres (NDCs) that receive goods from factories/production plants located in many different places, where the different products are "mixed" and then consolidated into loads, for delivery to customers.
*   Road transport companies have pallet networks which are used to combine goods from various suppliers into full loads for transhipment via a central hub onward to regional partners, who then, undertake the final delivery
*   Forwarding companies offer groupage/consolidation services between the UK to/from continental and global destinations

Inventory approaches

Vendor managed inventory (VMI)

VMI involves, suppliers holding stocks, at their customer's premises. It requires the sharing of information from customers, so that the supplier has visibility of the customer's demand and usage. Then, the supplier is able to control stock levels in the customer's premises and manages inventory for the customer; the supplier making all replenishment decisions, monitoring customer inventory levels and possibly directly processing customer demands. VMI can therefore be especially useful when there is stable demand.

Customer ownership and the payment to the supplier is only is made; when the stock has been used/sold. For the customer this clearly reduces costs, reduces the risks of buying goods that will not be used/sold and improves cash flows. For the supplier, VMI ties in the customer with longer term relationships; this however is at the expense of delayed payments and potential product returns.

Consignment Stocking

This is another arrangement where a supplier keeps stock on the customer's premises and the stock is only drawn upon when the customer needs materials for example; as with maintenance, repair and operating (MRO) items. The product remains in the ownership of the supplier and the ownership only passes at the time of use. Similar therefore to VMI, however the visibility of information and control of replenishment is different; this remaining with the user/buyer in consignment stocking. Consignment stock is therefore managed by the customer and not the supplier. This is the main difference with VMI where the supplier manages the stock. It is important to formalise an agreement between vendor/supplier and buyer/customer/user. This need to cover such aspects as:

*   What products are consigned?
*   Who is responsible for stock checking?
*   Length of the arrangements?
*   Who arranges insurance cover?
*   Who pays for damaged s whilst in stock?
*   When exactly when does ownership pass?
*   What happens to unused stocks?
*   How can the supplier get access for inspection and checking?

Co-managed inventory (CMI)

CMI involves joint working of suppliers with customers to satisfy demand by cooperatively, managing inventory; rather than handing the day to day management over totally to suppliers (as happens in VMI). It is cooperative approach, with information exchange using appropriate systems, like EPOS/EDI/E-mail, combined with, developing better relationships, such as using cross functional teams.

These effectively involve the customer outsourcing the stock holding. It will also involve collaboration; both topics that have already been discussed. VMI may involve the customer holding stock on their premises but this will be managed by the supplier, or, with CMI, the supplier holds specific levels of "reserved" stock, which are delivered as required by the customer (this is usually called consignment inventory as it is held "on consignment").

With VMI, the supplier controls the flow of inventory required to replenish their customers stock. To do this the supplier needs daily information from the customer's sales/usage activity as well as in the forecasting, if appropriate. There is therefore much similarity with CMI, which also involves both supplier and customer working together to jointly manage inventory. CMI has been trailed extensively in the UK grocery sector. Retailer Somerfield led a major trial from May 1995 until April 1996 with twelve branded suppliers (reported extensively: "The Effective Implementation of Co-Managed Inventory" in "Focus" September 1996). Somerfield provided rolling 39 week forecasts for each product based on the levels of daily deliveries from DCs, together with the previous two years sales data.

Closer collaboration led to a clearer understanding of each others motivations, objectives and constraints. Using a common IT network format the trial showed that CMI could deliver many of the benefits associated with VMI of lower inventories, improved availability and customer service. Guinness also in 1995 started CMI with Whitbread Brewery and reported reduced stock of around 30% during the first year of CMI.

As VMI and CMI involve the supplier more in the inventory management function, then an effective and trusted supplier is needed to ensure the continuity of supply at the right time with the right quantity. This will only be practical where collaboration approaches are used. The supplier will therefore need to be integrated into their customers business so that can monitor stock usage and then determine the appropriate supply. This integration may be through ICT visibility or by supplier being based on-site or by making regular visits to the customers' site.

The common themes therefore involved in VMI/CMI are:
- speedy data transmission between the customer and suppliers to enable goods to move more quickly from supply to demand sources
- the breakdown of functional barriers both internally and externally so that more effective supply is enabled
- information systems including bar codes, to allow all players to monitor demand consumption, control stock levels and coordinate supply to meet the demand
- delivery frequencies and timings that minimise stock holding

VMI and CMI will not therefore suit all supply/demand requirements or all supplier/customer situations, but where applicable, it can be a most effective strategy.

Financial approaches

Direct Product Profitability (DPP)

This is an accounting technique to allocate fixed costs direct to specific products. It therefore attempts to ensure that each SKU can be fully costed and compared to its selling price, so that profit can be specifically identified on a per SKU basis. It therefore removes any average costing, on say a percentage of cost basis allocation, that will often give distorted figures; especially when the range of price and cost variable is high. Essentially a tool used in retailing it can be viewed as the following:

Sales less the cost of goods sold
= Gross margin, plus allowances/discounts
= Adjusted gross margin
Less warehouse costs
Less transport costs
Less retailing costs
= DPP

DPP can also be used by suppliers who may wish to reduce their customers cost of ownership (TCO) (that we looked at this earlier in purchasing). Additionally, in allocating and working out costs correctly, then the earlier examined activity based costing (ABC) can be used.

Economic Value Added (EVA)

Like DPP and Activity Based Costing, this was developed to overcome weaknesses seen in traditional accounting practices. The concept is to deduct from the net operating profit, a charge for the amount of capital employed. A positive EVA therefore means that value is being created, a negative one that value is being wasted and destroyed.

EVA has some critics:

- Capital investment by organisations is reduced, so that the EVA remains more positive
- Use of capital is only one measure and it does not cover the other measures that contribute to profit, such as innovation, market standing, people development, productivity, utilisation of other resources, etc.
- Use of human capital and knowledge may actually be more critical than the financial capital of an organisation

Nevertheless, EVA can assist in showing more exactly where any financial capital costs focus needs to be.

Lean and Agile approaches

Lean

This represents efficiency and eliminating waste, by enhancing the flow between source/user to satisfy a known and predictable demand, for example, as with MRP and with J.I.T. in car manufacturing where suppliers are selected for product quality and reliability as well as the cost.

In the car industry, it can be seen as, concentrating more on the supply chain, with "stock push". Planning and forecasting can be the main driver, with Economic Batch Quantities/ Make to Stock production methods. It can take up to 18 hours to build a new car, yet, up to three months to get the car to consumer; therefore these post production times are being targeted under "the three day car" banner (this being the lead-time, from build to the consumer).

Lean can be seen as the response to dealing with, the perceived uncertainty in demand, therefore, efficient supply is undertaken. It is the supply side that is Lean; the demand side may however be "Fat."

Agile

As demand can be difficult to predict, there is therefore the need to have a rapid response to the end market demand. Demand drives the supply chain, for example as in Efficient Consumer Response (ECR) in food retailing where suppliers are selected on speed and flexibility as well as cost. With food retailers, they can be seen as concentrating more on the demand chain (or pipeline), with "demand pull". The end marketplace (the consumer), is the ultimate demand driver, therefore having such certainty, can enable Make (MTO) and Assemble to Order (ATO) production. In turn, this can also mean having modular product structures with postponement until the latest time possible, for example, customisation, kiting, and assembly in Distribution Centres (DCs).

Everything that is bought, produced, moved, and handled is in response to a known customer requirement.

Lean/Agile Conclusion

The main change needed to be agile is to get close to the market real time demand. Then all the other challenges will remain for efficient and effective Supply Chain Management, such as:

- creating value from the customers perspective
- identifying the value stream
- highlighting non value added work
- sharing information,
- process integration by smoothing the supply/demand chain,
- forming a network of companies who work closely together

These all remain, as important challenges and changes needed to the past "traditional" ways of supplying products to markets. Indeed for the Car industry, such challenges are conceptually similar to those initially experienced when they changed to J.I.T. supply from the previous bulk buying and large stock holding processes.

The agile and lean terms need not be mutually exclusive. Within a Total Supply Chain viewpoint therefore, being "Lean" and "Agile", is both efficient and effective, as both "sides" of Supply and Demand, respond by "pulling" to the end market consumer demands in real time. "Leagility" has been used to describe the combined lean and agile viewpoints.

Quality Management

Quality Management has many parallels with Supply Chain Management and is therefore very supportive in aims and ideals. Quality management represents the involvement and commitment of everyone, in continuously improving work processes, to satisfy the requirements and expectations of all internal and external customers. It is therefore fundamentally similar to Supply Chain management; as will be further seen in the ten basic principles of Quality Management:

- agreed customer requirements
- understand and improve customer/supplier chains
- do the right things
- do things right first time
- measure for success
- continuous improvement is the goal
- management must lead
- training is essential
- communicate more effectively
- recognise successful involvement

There are several options available to use to further these principles:

Kaizan means continuous improvement in a gradual and ordered way. It has an objective of the elimination of waste in the processes, components and functions. It has two parts: one being improvements and change and the other being to do this ongoing and continually.

Total Quality Management (TQM) is an approach towards larger scale company change and improves existing process and functions. TQM needs strong direction and leading from the top as it needs commitment and involvement from all. As such middle management in traditional command and control structures can often be a barrier to TQM, as the managers may fear a loss of control as their jobs become largely superfluous as now, involvement spreads "below" them.

Six Sigma involves statistics, as in the use of the word sigma, which is another word for standard deviation. Statistics are used to establish company benchmarks which assist in work processes being continually improved to meet the customers' expectations. It has a "goal" that the chance of failure is only 3.4 in a million opportunities (this is Six Sigma/standard deviations). Whilst this may be unattainable, it does indicate that Six Sigma, like Quality generally, represents often a "journey to a destination".

The six key concepts are:
- **Critical quality:** what actually is it that matters to the customer?
- **Defects:** where there is failure to deliver what the customer wants?
- **Process capability:** what can the processes do?
- **Variation:** what is the customer's perception and how does this differ from the critical quality?
- **Stable operations:** what has to be done to ensure consistent and certain processes?
- **Design for Six Sigma:** what is involved in designing to meet customer needs and to get process capability?

The seven wastes from Quality Management are as follows:
- overproduction
- waiting
- transporting
- inappropriate processing
- unnecessary inventory
- unnecessary/excess motion
- defects

These all have useful connections to performance improvements and are examined later.

Reverse Logistics

This may be defined as "the management of returns from users back to senders", "the management of returns from stores back to: the store for resale, to the supplier, to consumers through appropriate channels or for disposal" or as "closing the supply-chain loop by recapturing the value." The process involved is the collection - return to designated site - check the condition - collate - recover/disposal - redistribution.

The keys areas are as follows:
*   The technology/information to say "why" they are to be returned; for example, are they faulty are they damaged, are they not needed. (For example: clothing catalogue goods returns are 18 to 35%, electrical catalogue returns are 4 to 5% of despatched product)
*   Product ID, for example, the senders scanning and tagging, if any.
*   The process of coming back, the "how" (for example: collection by delivery vehicles, assessment, categorising)
*   The feedback and performance information (for example: to buyers/marketing). Life cycle product costing approaches of cradle to grave are emphasised here
*   The assessment on receipt and the disposal options (see below), and the space required to do this. This may be better being done offsite
*   The returns policy of the companies involved, for example: the supplier and the retailers policy may vary
*   The full financial implications of the process

Recovery & disposal options for reverse logistics:
Inspection is needed by "expert eyes". The basic options involved here are:
1. No change to the original state, therefore re-use and place back into stock.
2. Dismantle to re-use = recover/re-manufacture or re-furbish.
3. Extracting of elements to be used as raw material elsewhere = repair/reconditioning of damaged products; replace missing components, recover of packaging and product.
4. Return to supplier; perhaps for disassembly into parts for recycling
5. Disposal to landfill sites

These options then may involve re-stock, resale, scrap obsolete products/parts whilst, considering in all, the legal implications and environmental restrictions

The following case study illustrates a response to reverse logistics, of Third Party Company:

Case Study: Reverse logistics (WEEE) and Salvesen

Reverse logistics (RL) is an expression that we are going to hear a lot more about, particularly with the growth in home delivery services and legislation such as the WEEE directive.

The meaning of WEEE
The Waste Electrical and Electronic Equipment (WEEE) Directive affects anybody involved in manufacturing, selling, distributing, recycling or treating electrical and electronic equipment. It aims to reduce the waste arising from electrical and electronic equipment, and improve the environmental performance of those involved in.

Private householders will be able to return their WEEE to collection facilities free of charge, and producers (manufacturers, sellers, distributors) will be responsible for financing the collection, treatment, recovery and disposal of it. Producers will also be responsible for financing the management of WEEE from products placed on the market.

Later, producers will be required to achieve a series of recycling and recovery targets for different categories of appliance, and the UK must have reached an average WEEE collection rate of four kilograms for each private householder annually. It covers not just the return of faulty goods, but handling goods ordered by mistake, overstock items, display goods and also product recalls. It is an area with many pitfalls but also significant opportunities. Reverse logistics deals with not just the product itself; but also waste products and information about the product and customer. Many companies claim to have expertise in RL, but few can point to much substantial experience.

Relationship

One which can is Christian Salvesen, which has had a long relationship with Marks & Spencer in non-food distribution. Consumer development director David Hughes has some strong views on what makes it work — and what doesn't. "Unless you manage big ticket returns well you can severely dent the margin on sales," he says. For example, for full credit on a returned TV some manufacturers will demand not only the TV itself, but also the original box, the instructions, all the leads and the remote control. And there are more complex items still, such as PCs. Time is of the essence in returning these, says Hughes, "PCs are becoming obsolete in about four months now, although some components can be re-used."

The key to the relationship between supplier and retailer is the returns agreement (RA) — or often the no-returns agreement (NRA). An NRA is typical for imported goods — particularly those with a relatively short shelf-life like PCs — but a retailer should expect a higher level of discount. Alternatively, the RA may incorporate a returns quota — say no more than 2% of items may be returned. "While you had specialist electrical retailers selling electrical goods, they learned long ago how to deal with returns. But the supermarkets haven't got that luxury — and this also applies to the DIY market and furniture retailing."

Damaged

Furniture has its own problems. "It's so easily damaged, just like white goods. It has high handling costs, high cube, it is difficult to store and it is difficult to realise a value from it. Developing a secondary market in furniture is difficult — but I think we could get involved there. That's what we're trying to develop — a business where we can release the value for our customers."

Another area of returns is what Hughes calls Trading Standards returns — product recalls, for example. "Typically if retailers can return it they will — they take the path of least resistance," Hughes says.

One of the thorniest issues of reverse logistics is cost, and how one charges for it. Hughes suggests three options for charging:

- Open book
- Fixed price (but only if the level of returns can be very well predicted)
- Unitary pricing, with a sliding scale of charges. "As you scale up the efficiencies do improve," he says. "and returns handling lends itself to both dedicated and shared-user applications."

Waste, particularly packaging waste, is a considerable element of this, and Christian Salvesen runs the recycling and waste operations for all Tesco and Asda RDCs. The M&S account generates millions of plastic coat hangers, which are sold to a recycling company; conversely, the polypropylene intermediate bulk containers (IBCs) used by industrial liquids suppliers are often returned to the factory.

When handling returns, many of the same issues apply as in conventional retail logistics — shrinkage, for one. "You have to put in place the same sort of security measures you would in a distribution setup," he says.

But it is not just employees you have to watch for; customer fraud is rife too, particularly with electronic goods. With digital cameras, for example, customers will remove memory cards or rechargeable batteries, replacing them with defective or less desirable ones. Inkjet printers can have a full cartridge replaced with an empty one.

"People will buy a lawn- mower, go home, cut the grass and bring it back saying it won't work!" says Hughes. Dinner jackets are another item favoured by the "use once, and then return" consumer. "Manufacturers may dispute return credits if a product works — and they will tell you that a high proportion of products returned have no fault." So an RL contractor has to be a broker and a policeman as well as a returns processor.

"This is more like manufacturing: it's a processing centre rather than a warehouse — it's a flow-through process. As a logistics company we are good at this". Hughes himself has a background in manufacturing — primarily brewing — so he is used to process management and product flow.

Batches

And one of the things Salvesen is manufacturing is information — lots of it. Handling batches of hundreds or thousands of items at a time is not enough. "You need to deal with everything at item level — identify product number, identify the store that sent it, and even attach customer information."

Building customer relation ships is a given now, even a cliché, but it isn't easy — especially when a large superstore may have 60,000 regular customers. "There is some specialisation in the IT needed for this — you cannot use a warehouse management system alone. There are only a few IT systems in the world we've found that can do this job."

US-sourced systems are not necessarily suited to UK operations — US and UK retailing is still quite different — and they can be expensive. "Some US companies quote up to £1 million for an installation," says Hughes. Nevertheless, the US is ahead of us in some aspects of RL — not least the setting up of national returns centres.

Retailer

But the WEEE directive is not an entirely known quantity yet. "Every country is now interpreting it... the details are not fixed at all. Retailers are hoping they won't have too many responsibilities — it might make some retailers think about whether they want to import directly."

The economics of recycling are likely to change, too. "Some retailers are putting goods into a skip in store — when WEEE comes in they will be in breach". However, Hughes emphasises that he doesn't want to get involved in every aspect of goods processing. "We'll be an enabler, not a repairer or reseller".

So how has Christian Salvesen approached the issue of reverse logistics? Hughes sees it in terms of the physical processing of goods, credit recovery and the duty of care for disposal. The purely physical side of returns processing costs a lot, but benefits enormously from economies of scale, according to Hughes. "To process an outbound item through an RDC typically costs 10 pence. Some retailers manage returns in stores: we've costed it at more than £20 an item; in a central pro cessing centre, that cost can be reduced to somewhere between 80p and £2. But it's a much higher cost than an RDC because everything has to be dealt with as a single item."

While the physical processing is far from trivial, "the real added value is in these last two. The skill set to do the second group is definitely here", he says. "We're building intellectual capital," Hughes adds. "For instance, we've built relationships with secondary markets." Examples of these are auctioneers, charities and jobbing firms, which can dispose of items in other countries. Hughes believes that this experience is particularly valuable in competition with other firms which claim RL expertise. "We'll have an eye for the deal that they don't have," he says, pointing out that "jobbers can be swamped — then you can end up with unsellable stock. The important thing is to keep shifting the stock. You can't sit on the stuff — its value is dropping all the time," he says.

Reputation

It is vital, however, to think about brand value at all times. "As a retailer you've got to worry about your reputation, about where your product is being sold off."

There are specialist areas within RL; for instance, home entertainment products such as DVDs. Handling a huge number of items when they are launched means that a significant number of them will be unsold, and will have to be discounted — or destroyed. David Hughes is convinced that reverse logistics will be a massive issue, brought to prominence by legislation. "I think this market is just about to break;

everybody's been talking it up, but the WEEE directive is moving things along. That what's concentrating minds."

Source: Motor Transport 17 July 2003 "Return to Sender"

Collaborative Supply Chains

As has been noted many times in this section, collaboration is an underlying theme in many of the approaches and methods. Indeed, as we have already stated, the optimum and the "ideal" in Supply Chain Management will only ever be found by working and collaborating fully with all and as also has been earlier noted, the change from transactional methods to collaborative approaches goes far beyond the technical issues, of say ICT connectivity, and fully embraces the soft skills.

Supply chain management collaboration between companies, where determined as being appropriate, will not succeed without appropriate recognition that soft skill development is required.

The barriers to collaboration can be viewed as follows:

Barriers	Comments
No trust	Fear here is usually of giving information to competition
Poor communications	Usually meaning there is no up to date sharing and also a comment on the format of communication being used
No "big picture" view	Too focused on "own" issues and problems
No risk taking	Fear of having "all eggs in one basket" and a preference for "playing off"
Prefer power based adversary transactional approach	Annual contracts and three quotes, common in the public sector, this continues to perpetuate adversary approaches
Want quick and short term wins	In reality success will depend on time and effort over longer periods
No sharing of benefits	The power view of "keeping it all" whereas all should save from mutual collaborations.
No planning, all "kick and rush" rules	Collaboration is hard work involving soft skills. It also will need adequate planning
No support for any changing "how we do things"	Top support is important
"Output is king and anyway, we are too busy fire-fighting"	Concentration here is on the "operations" and looking just for short term efficiency whilst ignoring longer term effectiveness.
Fear of change	Remaining with the "status quo" in times of change and stable turbulence that is like the ostrich analogy of burying the head in the sand.
Fear of failure from the existing blame culture	Change to a "gain" culture is needed.

The benefits of collaboration in the supply chain have been noted as follows:

Aspect	Collaboration brings
Forecast accuracy	Increased external visibility will force better accuracy
Lead time	Reductions following sharing and joint improvements
Inventory	Reduced as stock levels fall
Utilisation of resources	Improved in a "leaner" operation with less waste
Costs	Reduced and improved
Service levels	Increased and improved
People	Trust and improved relationships

Rules of collaboration are that real and recognised benefits must be found for all internal and external players. This will involve:

- Business process integration at all stages
- Support collaboration of all the supply chain components
- Recognition of the culture(s)
- The importance of people relationships and when improving relationships it is useful to remember that:
    - "It is the soft stuff that is the hard stuff"
    - "People may be physically present, but are they there psychologically?"
    - "Only when all people come together is found the power of one"

It is people that change a company and it is the people who make the relationships in and between companies. In changing company culture ("what is done around here"), then this will need therefore to pass through the following stages:

Aspect	"Stormy/Blame"	"Steady/Sane"	"Sunny/Gain"
Goals	Announced	Communicated	Agreed
Information	Status symbol and power based	Traded	Abundant
Motivation	Manipulative	Focused on staff needs	A clear goal
Decisions	From above	Partly delegated	Staff take them
Mistakes	Are only made by staff	Responsibility is taken	Are allowed as learning lessons
Conflicts	Are unwelcome and "put down"	Are mastered	Source of new innovation
Control	From above	Partly delegated	Fully delegated
Management Style	Authoritarian/ aggressive	Cooperative	Participative/ assertive
Authority	Requires obedience	Requires cooperation	Requires collaboration
Manager	Absolute ruler and feels superior	Problem solver and decision maker	Change strategist and self confident

Once the culture has been defined, this will need the examination of all internal and external relationships. Trust will often remain a major barrier; however, without trust, there will be no relationship.

Trust is fundamentally about "having to give up, to another, what you personally believe is valuable to you", it is "One for all and all for one" and it is a "willing interdependence."

Trust is firstly built between people, one on one, and is not something that is built remotely between nebulous companies. The following is therefore involved when building trust "one-on-one":

- Doing what you say you will do
- Going beyond conventional expectations
- Undertaking open and honest communicating
- Being patient
- Accepting and admitting to mistakes
- Ensuring the other party gets a fair outcome.

Collaboration therefore is basically sharing together and involves:

- Shared goals = common purpose, collective commitment, agreeing the business we are in
- Shared culture = agreed values that bind us together, working cooperatively to the common goal
- Shared learning = pooling talent, skills, knowledge, reflecting, reviewing, revising and changing together
- Shared effort = one approach with flexible teams
- Shared information: the right information is shared with the right people for the right reasons, where the:
  - Right information is that used to give better service and reduce costs
  - Right people are those who can use it to help you
  - Right reasons is that which will "reduce, save, improve, quicker" etc.

(Source: Partnerships with People)

Supplier relationships

The following supplier relationships can be noted:

Relationship	Examples of Procurement methods used
Transactional	Competitive tendering and spot buying
Co-operative	Negotiation and preferred suppliers with framework agreements
Collaborative	Open book and joint working towards continuous improvements

The change from more arm's length transactional relationships to closer working collaborative relationships can also reflect a move towards more adaptive and effective supply chains. It will also involve different levels of trust, shown overleaf as levels one to three.

Level one trust	Level two trust	Level three trust
Boundary trust	Reliable trust	Goodwill trust
Contractual	Competence	Commitment
Explicit promises	Known standards	Anything that is required to foster the relationship
Standard performance	Satisfactory performance	Success beyond expectation
Mistakes bring enforcement	⟹	Mistakes give shared learning for advantage
Exchange data for transactions	Cooperate on information for mutual access	Cognitive connections and joint decision making
Animal brain	⟹	Human brain
Symbonic	Share	Swap
Time bound (as far as the contract says)	⟹	Open-ended, ongoing and leaving a legacy

However many people will not subscribe to such a mutually sharing collaborative supply chain management approach.

A major reason for this is that business is founded on power, for example as shown in the following:

- "Anger (from suppliers) at unreasonable demands, unsustainable prices and the rejection of high quality produce," by a supermarket company (Sandra Bell).
- The *Mail on Sunday* alleges the Retailer was asking 700 of its suppliers for a contribution from their contracts and the company was to lengthen its payments terms from 60 to 90 days. (*Supply Management* 18 January 2007)
- "The Company is locked in a bitter dispute battle with its suppliers over attempts to extract cost savings from its supply chain…One supplier claimed the company were arrogantly out of touch." (*Sunday Times* 11 February 2007)

Therefore two way collaboration can sit here as an uneasy concept; it is easy to "beat up" on someone when you have some power over their business/life. Another major reason for the lack of two way collaborative approaches is also that soft skills are the hard skills for many people in business as "we have been taught to compete; nobody has taught us to work together." (Alan Waller).

Power

Relationships between buyers and sellers will vary; power is not always equally distributed. For example buyers have power when:

- They have a high spend
- They are a large company with a good reputation that sellers desire to be associated with
- They are a growing developing company with future potential
- They have a large market share and influence
- The supplier market is very competitive

Meanwhile sellers have power where:
*   There are barriers to entry for other suppliers into their market, for example, requirements for specialised research and development
*   They have "unique" products. For example, OEM spare parts
*   They are monopoly or oligopoly; the association of power to monopoly or competition markets is shown further below:

Feature	Monopoly	Oligopoly	"Perfect" competition
Supply & Demand Control	Statutory	Fewer companies, with the possibility of market collusions	No controls, all open
Barriers to entry	Retained and look to maintain "status quo"	High costs to enter the market for "new" suppliers	Few to no barriers and low costs to enter
Market view	Focus and concentrate.	Large and valuable markets. Possible cartels	Customers can easily "switch." Continual search for providing what is required and needed.
Customers view	No really considered as they have no choice	Sometimes	Customer "rules"
Prices	Can charge "What the market will bear"	Stable and related to costs and desired profits. Possible price fixing.	Demand driven, possible cost plus provision.
Examples	Some oil companies	UK Supermarkets	UK Car assembly

The relative power dominance, between buyers and suppliers, can be further seen as follows:

With the buyer dominant:
*   There is often a small number of big buyers who buy a large percentage of a sellers output
*   It is easy for buyer to switch as there are many sources of supply
*   Low transaction costs
*   "Take it or leave it" approach.

With the seller dominant:
*   There is often a small number of big sellers who supply to many buyers
*   It is difficult for buyers to switch as there are few sources of supply
*   High transaction costs
*   They can "enforce"

With such relative levels of dominance, then this leads to unequal power distributions; these can be seen as a foundation for the forming of adversarial relationships. Using the Kraljic portfolio, we can see for example, the buyer's behaviour may be as follows (overleaf):

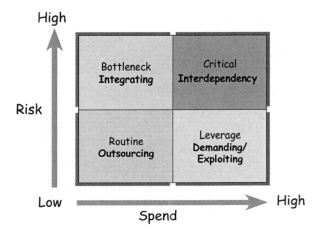

In turn; the link to more collaborative approaches maybe seen as follows:

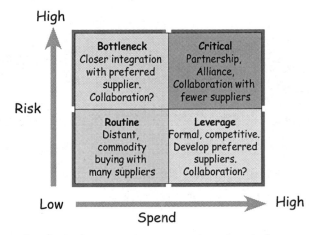

In turn, related to risks, we can see a strategic and tactical approach to procurement forming, as follows:

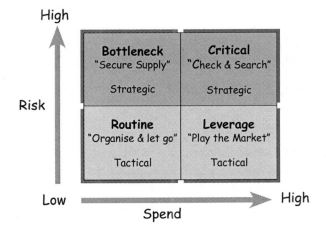

From this we can then see that there are actually varied levels of trust, openness and information exchange that results in varied types of relationships involved:

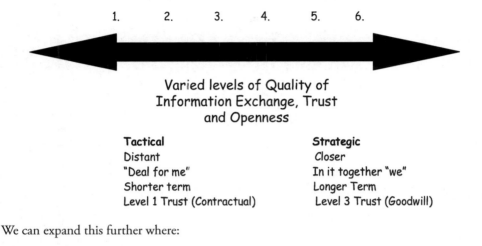

Varied levels of Quality of
Information Exchange, Trust
and Openness

Tactical	**Strategic**
Distant	Closer
"Deal for me"	In it together "we"
Shorter term	Longer Term
Level 1 Trust (Contractual)	Level 3 Trust (Goodwill)

We can expand this further where:

Tactical procurement uses the new trainee and junior buyers and has the following types of relationships:
1. Adversary relationships; "Take it or leave it"
2. Transactional relationships; Normal ordering
3. Single Source relationships; Exclusive agreements usually at fixed price for a specific time

Strategic procurement uses the more senior buyers with the following types of relationships:
4. Strategic alliance relationships; Working together for a specific purpose
5. Collaborative relationships; Commitment with shared risks/benefits
6. Co-destiny relationships; Interdependency

Relating this back to Kraljic, then the following gives us an ideal typical perspective:

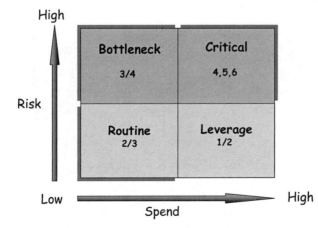

Keeping in our ideal typical view, then we can recap on the following stereotypes between transactional and collaborative approaches.

Transactional relationships have the following characteristics::
- Short term
- Separated/arms length
- Wiifm, what is in it for me ("I-me)
- "One off"
- Low contact/closed
- Little trust
- Price dominates
- "One night stand"
- Power based
- Win/loose
- One way (customer demands sensitive data)
- Customer keeps all cost savings
- All risk with supplier, customer risks zero
- Power based "spin"
- Adversarial and inefficient
- Hierarchical /superior subordinate
- Blame culture
- High formal controls
- Rigid contracts
- Alienated employees
- Predatory
- Technical Performance prescriptive specifications "rule"

Whereas collaborative relationships are typified by the following:
- Long term
- Close/alliance
- Wiifu, what is in it for us
- "For ever"
- Shared vision/open
- Trust/risk/benefits
- Shared destiny
- "Marriage"
- Equality based
- Win/win
- Two way exchange of sensitive data
- Mutual to reduce costs, times and waste
- Shared risk and benefits
- Pragmatic trust
- Challenging to implement and continue with
- Equality
- Problem solving culture
- Self controlled
- Flexible contracts
- Motivated employees

- Proactive
- Work beyond just "one" technical view

What fundamentally will have to be changed when following a collaborative approach? Well this topic has been more fully covered in *"The Relationship Driven Supply Chain"* by Emmett & Crocker (2006).

Meanwhile the following case studies give some very practical and useful examples of collaboration:

Case Study: 1992 Offshore Engineering and CRINE

In 1992, the UK offshore oil and gas engineering industry in the North Sea faced a crisis when the price of oil dropped to from $35 to $12 a barrel, making exploration uneconomic. Platform operators, contractors and suppliers came together to form the Cost Reduction Initiative for the New Era or CRINE; a cooperative effort to find ways of reducing wasteful activity in platform construction.

Alter 12 months of investigation and analysis the CRINE Report was published, recommending:
- functional rather than prescriptive specifications'
- common working practices
- non-adversarial contracts
- use of alliances
- reduction in bureaucracy
- a single industry body for pre-qualification

These recommendations were put into practice by industry. As a result the cost of oil and gas developments was reduced by 40%.

An unexpected result was the emergence of a network of innovative individuals committed to on-going co-operation for further improvement. By 1997 CRINE had been transformed into the CRINE Network, a continuous agent for change and a brand-name for cost reduction and competitiveness in the oil industry. Its vision is "People working together to make the UK oil and gas industry competitive anywhere in the world by the year 2000."

CRINE remains a model of "co-operative effort" in the supply chain which has been emulated and copied in many parts of the world. It has usefully been extended, through the ACTIVE Engineering Construction Initiative to the UK's process plant industries, with a view to improving efficiency and enhancing competitiveness.

Source: Rethinking Construction 1998

Case Study: Oil and Gas: The Supply Chain Code of Practice, 2002

This outlines a set of best practice guidelines for the UK oil and gas industry to:
*   Improve performance
*   Eliminate unnecessary costs
*   Add value and boost performance

First adopted by the industry in 2002, signatories undertake to work towards full compliance. They include major purchasers (Oil and Gas operators and principal contractors) and suppliers (companies providing goods or services). The Code applies to three key stages within the commercial process:

1. Plan
Transparent planning of contracting activity by major purchasers to improve supply chain capability.

Major purchasers
*   Communicate forward plans to the industry including areas and types of activity, expected contract value and timing.
*   Support the annual industry Share Fair where major purchasers communicate future plans and internal contacts to the Supply Chain.
*   Publicise a list of internal contacts to facilitate discussion around future plans with the contracting community. Maintain up-to- date First Point Assessment Limited (FPAL) Purchaser Profile including "how to do business with us" guidance, a contacts list and information on forward plans.

Suppliers
*   Review Purchaser plans, FPAL Purchaser Profiles and attend Industry Share Fairs to understand future requirements.

2. Contract
Streamline pre-qualification, tendering and negotiation processes to reduce bidding costs, eliminate waste, add value and increase competitiveness.

Major Purchasers
*   Where pre-qualification data is required only invite bids from suppliers registered with FPAL with an up-to-date capability assessment.
*   Eliminate supplier data duplication by utilising FPAL throughout the tender process.
*   Use industry standard ITT Models where appropriate. These embody fair contracting principles, encourage participation, invite bidders to demonstrate where they can add value, define value-based award criteria, outline timeframes and avoid data duplication.

- Provide appropriate de-briefing for all bids.
- Use industry standard contract forms where available (LOGIC type or company-specific global contracts), minimising amendments or additional terms and conditions.
- Include payment terms of 30 days in all contracts.

Suppliers
- Keep FPAL records valid and up-to-date, with Capability
- Assessments where required by purchasers.
- Refer purchasers to FPAL if duplicate information is requested.
- Participate in the Industry Mutual Hold Harmless as appropriate to company activity.
- Use standard industry contracts (LOGIC type or company- specific global contracts) minimising amendments or additional terms and conditions.

3. Perform and Pay
Increase feedback dialogue and shorten payment cycles to improve performance.

Major Purchasers
- Include performance indicators in all significant contracts with an appropriate review programme for the life of the contract.
- Give FPAL performance feedback at appropriate stages during the contract to improve mutual performance, minimise waste, learn from mistakes and best practice, and report on the extent of Code compliance achieved by both parties.
- Pay all valid invoices within 30 days.

Suppliers
- Track and discuss key contract performance indicators
- Request and participate in FPAL performance feedback, including assessment of Purchasers' performance.
- Submit complete and valid invoices with supporting documentation in a timely manner.
- Adopt a prompt payment policy for own suppliers.

Source: www.pilottaskforce.co.uk

Case Study: A Fruitful Partnership: effective partnership working: The Audit Commission

The Audit Commission use the term 'partnership' to describe a joint working arrangement where the partners::
- are otherwise independent bodies;
- agree to co to achieve a common goal;

- create a new organisational structure or process to achieve this goal, separate from their own organisations;
- a plan and implement a jointly agreed programme, of-ten with joint staff or resources;
- a share relevant information; and
- pool risks and rewards

The key points are:

Deciding to go into partnership
1. Does this organisation have clear and sound reasons for being involved in its current partnerships?
2. Where new partnerships must be set up to meet national requirements, what groundwork is being done locally to maximise their chances of success?
3. Are changes in behaviour or in decision-making processes needed to avoid setting up partnerships with only limited chances of success?

Getting started
4. Have all the partnerships in which the organisation is involved been reviewed to evaluate whether the form of the partnership is appropriate to its functions and objectives?
5. Do all the partnerships have an appropriately structured board or other decision-making forum?
6. When setting up a new partnership, how are prospective partners identified?

Operating efficiently and effectively
7. Do partners share the same main objectives for the partnership?
8. Are the partnership's objectives consistent with those of the partnership organisation?
9. If an outsider watched a partnership operate, would they be able to identify the partnership's main objectives?
10. Do the partners know where the boundaries between the activities of the partnership and of their own organisations lie?
11. Do the members of partnership steering groups have sufficient authority to commit their organisations to decisions?
12. Are partnerships prepared to delegate responsibility for parts of their work to particular partners?
13. Do large partnerships have an executive group that all the partners trust to make decisions on their behalf?
14. Are project-planning techniques used to ensure the separate agreement of all the partners to a course of action in good time, when necessary?
15. Do the partnership's decisions get implemented effectively?
16. Are partnership staff selected for their technical competence and for their ability to operate both inside and outside a conventional public sector framework?
17. What actions are taken to build and maintain trust between partners?

18. If members have dropped out of a partnership, what lessons have been learnt about how to maintain involvement in the future?

Reviewing success
19. Does each partnership have a shared understanding of the outcomes that it expects to achieve, both in the short and longer term?
20. What means have been identified for measuring the partnership's progress towards expected outcomes and the health of the partnership itself?
21. Has the partnership identified its own performance indicators and set jointly agreed targets for these?
22. Are the costs of the partnership known, including indirect and opportunity costs?
23. Are these costs actively monitored and weighed against the benefits that the partnership delivers?
24. What steps have been taken to make sure that partnerships are accountable to the individual partners, external stakeholders, service users and the public at large?
25. Are some or all of the partnership's meetings open to the public?
26. Is information about the partnership's spending, activities and results available to the public?
27. Does the partnership review its corporate governance arrangements?
28. Has the partnership considered when its work is likely to be complete, and how it will end/handover its work when this point is reached?

Source: The Audit Commission: A Fruitful Partnership: effective partnership working

With collaboration, the "how to get there" is not going to be easy. The following section on "re-thinking" tells us why this may be.

Supply Chain Re-thinking

Many people do understand what is involved when following a supply chain approach. However, ensuring the supply chain is optimised for the benefits of all participants will often mean a re-thinking of traditional ways.

Such re-thinking may not be an easy process for some individuals in some companies and this may therefore limit the optimum development of supply chains. It would seem a possibility that Supply Chain development in the UK may well falter because of the prevalent way of management thinking. What however is sure is that, what worked for many years, may not work for many more.

Supply Chain Development

Supply chains can be at various stages of development and the following gives a view of possible developments (see overleaf):

Stage	Structure of the supply chain	Some actions needed
"Starting out"	Fragmented and uncoordinated. Low cost/service levels, high stock levels	Internal alignments. Coordinate external suppliers. Measure supply chain efficiency.
"Getting there"	Some working together but still high stock levels.	Supply chain structure. ICT systems internal/ external for transparency/visibility
"Arrived?"	Has a supply chain structure but have slow growth and competition increasing.	Develop new sales channels. Modular products. Direct delivery to customers. Integrate fully the ICT systems
"Re-birth"	Static market growth	Increased out sourcing. Strengthen existing relationships, Branding, R&D, marketing
"Starting out again"	Virtual structures	Active monitoring and remain flexible for the "next" changes

Changes when using a Supply Chain approach

The supply chain approach will require changes to "the way we do thing around here". The following briefly illustrates some of the needed changes:

Changes	Some of the needed "ends" are:
"Silo" functions to "holistic" processes	Decision integration, organisations of extended enterprises, collaborative management approaches, web connected, real time focus
Product "sells" to Customer "buys"	Demand pull, order driven, low to zero stock holding, involved suppliers, short production runs, real time visibility, short product life cycles, fewer suppliers, market segmentation
Transactions to relationships	Dependency , commitment, cooperation, collaboration, aligned company cultures, extensive trust, proactive management

The way we look

Taking a Supply Chain approach will require a business to change and this, in turn, will mean changing the thinking from a current and known position, towards a possibly unknown but planned for future. As the way we think affects what we do, then the way we think, is an important process to be considered.

Research suggests our brain is in two parts - the left hemisphere and the right hemisphere. At least, this is the simple view - front and back, upper and lower quadrants are other "divisions". Indeed, research into brain activity, continues to contribute to our understanding at a rapid pace. Meanwhile, the left and right view suggests we have a Logical Left side Brain and a Creative Right side Brain. The Left side brain will firstly conduct an Analysis, will then Act, and finally will Feel (for example, is the action "correct" and "right"). The right side brain however, works the other way, Feeling, then Action, then Analysis.

Most people are relatively flexible in this brain wiring and of course the influences of environmental forces and the way we are nurtured, treated, handled etc, also has a powerful impact to our thinking and to our personal behaviour. In exploring simply the left side/right side brain differences, then the following is revealed:

Logical left brain side people	Creative right side brain people
Prefer written, mathematical, science based approaches	Prefer musical, art/visual based approaches
Objective, linear thinking, short term views	Subjective, wholes/parallel processing, longer term views
Analytical, step by step "head" thinkers	Creative, free flowing "heart" thinkers
Rational "facts" based reasoning that converges	Emotional "feelings" synthesis that diverges
Summary: Analyses-acts-feels	Summary: Feels-acts-analyses

Most individuals can usefully recognise which side is their personally representative one.

The way companies manage

As companies are collections of individuals; it is therefore possible to see left side and right companies. Following on from the above individual brain sided view, then companies may be viewed as follows:

Left brain influenced companies	Right brain influenced companies
Task based "today."	People based and a long term view.
Problems reoccur as only the symptoms are treated; ("Elastoplast" solutions).	Problems are tackled by looking at the thinking that causes the problems.
Making/selling products-services has the priority.	Make people before the products-services.
The way forward is with Science/technology.	The way forward is by Motivating/empowering people.
"The numbers speak for themselves."	"It is how we connect together that is important."
Incremental results/parts.	Holistic, whole results/parts.
More Western cultural base	More Eastern and Latin cultural base

Left sided companies will often work with fixed assumptions for development and growth as they are incapable of "going outside of the box". When they are pushed to change from "tradition", they will react negatively as they fundamentally believe the way forward is "more of the same." They would see the only solution, for example to company growth, as needing a bigger share of the existing market.

Supply Chain thinking

The ways of thinking will also translate into company management approaches, for "as a person thinks then so they are" (Proverbs 23.7). This way of thinking includes how supply chains are managed and structured. The following diagrams represent a thought process for the past and future of Supply Chain management.

1) Older Approach/Linear thinking

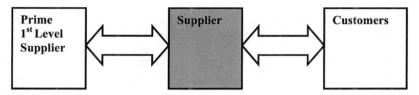

This model has given proven benefits, as will be shown later, to the previous non-supply chain ways of functional silo management.

It will be seen that this approach represents linear thinking, which is classically left brain mode. This approach is also the major model currently used in the UK for supply chain development. By following the above left brain explanations, we can see that this means having short term task centred approaches with an incremental view of the supply chain, with relationships to the next level only. This may or may not involve a collaborative approach and will more than likely have fixed arrangements and contracts in place. It will tend to use a rigid and reactive approach to customer service with scheduled and rational replenishment.

The supplier may also feel that the supply chain coordination's are all one way and that "coercive power" is being used; this being noted for example as "the bullying and exploitation in which supermarkets indulge" (L. Michaels, March 2004).

2) Newer approach/Network thinking.
Here there is some attempt to go further into the supply chain using collaborative approaches and extending beyond the first supplier level. Fixed arrangements with boundaries/contracts may exist but the collaboration will be more open and sharing. Customer service can be more responsive and flexible with real time replenishments.

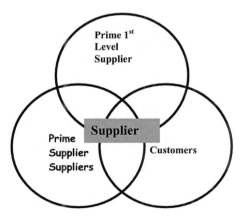

3) Emerging Approach/Systems Thinking

In this model, much more fluid arrangements occur, with systems thinking recognising the complex interactions that affect each other player in the specific supply chain. Right brain thinking concentrates on the wholes of the supply chain and perhaps uses seamless collaboration and virtual arrangements. Collaboration will be totally open and shared, and is unbound and innovative. Each specific supply chain could be viewed as a small company in itself comprising of cross internal functions and jointly managed with suppliers/customers, maybe following a matrix/project management structure organised into specific supply chain cells with decentralised control and shared responsibility from all involved.

This follows the basic principles of "small within big" that has for example, worked successfully when adopting TQM and JIT methods for production cells internally within product manufacturing/assembly organisations. Interestingly, such approaches were pioneered in Japan, a more natural right brain culture but of course have since been actively adopted and managed in the UK culture. Some changing in thinking therefore went on.

A summary of the three models on supply chain thinking follows:

Old Supply Chain approach	Newer Supply Chain approach	Emerging Supply Chain approach
Linear thinking	Network thinking	Systems "links and loops" thinking
Maybe collaborative at first level only	Collaborative and maybe beyond first levels	Collaborative and seamless in scope
Fixed contractual arrangements at "arms length"	Fixed arrangements/ boundaries/contracts	Virtual arrangements, unbound and innovative
Horizontal flow chart shape.	Venn shape.	Petal/Shamrock shape.
"Rigid"	"Connected"	"Fluid"

129

Changing how we think

Companies can be slow to change their thinking and there have been many well known examples of former company sector leaders who have slipped from the number one position and also there are examples of former state owned monopoly companies that no longer exist. In Supply Chain management, the consequence of "sticking to the knitting" thinking can be as follows:

- Adversary play offs with suppliers
- Long production runs of not needed products
- "Just in case" expensive stock holding
- Customers get fed up and go elsewhere
- Inspection, reworking, warranty claims
- Vertical silo management structures
- "Turf conscious" reactive "fire fighting" managers
- "Rowing the boat" upstream and resisting change

Companies are a collection of individuals and it is the thinking of the individuals in companies that needs to change. As has been noted above, individuals will tend to be more "happy" in one of the brain sides. This then means they can miss out on the other side. To be complete, we therefore need both sides. This is the classic whole brain thinking. Clearly many companies do of course, try to reflect such whole brain thinking through their recruitment policies and in the way they structure the organisation of the business.

But for efficient and effective supply chain management then perhaps, companies and the individuals in companies need to take more conscious responsibility for the thinking. Business channels change and when taking the view that supply chains now compete, this can mean thinking in a different way. Those individuals/companies who do not do this, may well find that they will not be "invited to the party" in the future. An example here is where a supply chain approach acknowledges that supplier numbers will be reduced; yet, some suppliers will maintain a "head in the sand" ostrich incremental approach, perhaps believing the reductions could not possibly affect them.

Thinking differently

Our brain is actually very similar to everyone else's, but the difference comes from, how we use it. Individuals and companies should be challenged to use the brain differently.

If they are more on the "creative right" side, then the need is to be more of a "logical left". The following could be tried:

As Individuals	For Companies
Be on time for appointments.	Keep promises and commitments.
Practice and plan a step/step approach.	Get the parts and processes working well, together
Time plan each step.	Use time based KPIs.
Have a work space that is ordered and structured.	Reorganise the flows in the supply chain.

If more of a "logical left" side, then the need is to be more of a creative right. The following could be tried:

As Individuals	For Companies
Brainstorm to create ideas.	Look at the whole supply chain beyond first level suppliers
Make visual mind map notes to enable free flowing visual images.	Make a supply chain map of the business and its supply chains
Explore a new neighbourhood.	Explore how to get the people relationships "right"
Try and understand your pet's feelings.	Try to understand how the staff "feel"

The Future: the right or the left sided company?

The optimum and the whole will only of course be found by using parts from all sides of the brain. The concern however is that remaining with traditionally British left side thinking that this will very likely mean that the trends and ways forward for supply chain management are never realised. This can mean, for example missing a future of:

- A few long term suppliers and joint action teams in the whole supply chain
- Short production runs with quick changeovers
- Minimal stockholding, JIT type supply through the supply chain
- Being able to serve more demanding customers
- Obtaining right first time quality throughout the supply chain
- Having process and flatter cross functional management structures
- Empowered proactive firelighting managers
- Continuous improvement and change

The way of thinking and the way the supply chain is structured and managed are therefore critical. The reported benefits of following a supply chain approach have been documented earlier; it will be noted that different approaches give significantly different results:

	No Supply Chain: Functional Silos	Internal Integrated Supply Chain	Plus, External Integration to the first level only
Inventory days of supply Indexed	100	78	62
Inventory carrying cost % sales	3.2%	2.1%	1.5%
On time in Full deliveries	80%	91%	95%
Profit % Sales	8%	11%	14%

It will be seen that by following a supply chain approach, then the inventory costs fall, profit and the service fulfilment increases; the "best of both worlds" for the company undertaking the approach. This is why supply chain approaches have been actively pursued by those companies looking for lower costs and improved service levels; it is very clear therefore that supply chain management "works".

What is also especially interesting here is that the structure of the supply chain is shown. Furthermore, the network thinking supply chain that goes beyond first level suppliers and the systems thinking one, should both indicate savings beyond those of the supply chains that stop at the first level integration.

But many companies will choose consciously to remain with the power based "winner takes all" supply chain approaches of the adversarial pursuit of "value for me alone" and will remain content with dealing at the first level only. This clearly may be appropriate and be seen as good business when the measure of success remains with profit for me alone.

However, in a future of market driven forces and increased uncertainty, one wonders how long companies having old established structures and holding such one sided views will survive, without re-structuring internally and without having to find new strengths externally beyond themselves. Releasing the strengths of collaboration and cooperation externally will arguably only happen when all the players will also get a benefit.

Thinking differently and looking for more creative and innovative ways to manage the supply chain may therefore be a future only a few companies are able to undertake. For example, moving to more collaborative approaches involves win/win and involves trust. This remains a most difficult aspect for those left sided rational thinking companies who prefer to use the German word for partnership of partnershaft.

It would seem a possibility that Supply Chain development in the UK may well falter because of the prevalent way of management thinking. There is a Welsh saying that says; "adversity comes with learning in its hand". It could be painful to wait for the adversity and the associated hard lessons of learning from mistakes. One thing is very sure; what worked for many years may not work for many more. Therefore there is a real challenge to learn anew and in so doing, to change. Learning and changing are indelibly connected; you cannot have one without the other.

Trade-offs

Taking a more holistic view with all players across the supply chain(s) means examining the Total Cost /Service balance and will involve trade-offs. This means deciding what has the priority; therefore a decision has to be taken, for example:
- Time; how much, how urgent etc?
- Cost; how much, how can cost be saved etc?
- Quality; what standard are we measuring against etc?
- Quantity: how many, what type etc?

When we look wider, that greater possibilities are found. An example here is making an overall reduction in costs, whilst the service levels increase and the following example shows the effects of changes that were made in one supply chain between a supplier and their customer. From an

original cost base line of 100% then:
- Raw materials costs fell to 71.5 %
- Production costs increased to 115.6%
- Finished goods stock costs reduced to 66.4 %
- Transport costs increased to 102.8%
- Total costs were reduced to 97.3%
- Service levels increased from 90 to 98%

Whilst some individual costs increased, the overall costs decreased. Meanwhile the service was improved. We cannot imagine that the people in change of Production and Transport would have sponsored such a change on their own. Unless a total more holistic supply chain trade-off view was taken between the two companies, then such double wins on cost and service improvements may not have been found.

Trade-offs are possible in three basic ways:

(1)Within a function

Procurement   Production   Logistics   Marketing

(2)Between functions

(3) Between Companies

1) Within functions, for example:
- Cost paid v product quality
- Cost paid v product availability
- Cost v service between air v sea freight

2) Between functions, for example:
- Purchase price v Total Acquisition Cost
- Stock holding v J.I.T supply
- Production cost in the above example of 115.6% v total costs of 97.3%

3) Between Companies, for example:
- Transactional v Collaborative supply
- Dependable v Ad hoc supply
- In the above example, a cost reduction of 2.7% v the service increase of 8%

133

Trade-offs are fundamental and a basic "tool" in Supply Chain Management. Indeed, an early 1990s UK supply chain department in one large company I worked with, was internally known as "the department of trade-offs".

Throughout this book we have seen many examples of trade-offs and identified many areas where they are needed. There are therefore many possibilities and opportunities available to integrate/Coordinate/Control across the supply chain(s) networks, starting by "winning the home games first" in and between the internal functions; then followed by all external connections to the supply chain networks, nationally, internationally and globally.

Information and the supply chain

Information is required for every stage of the supply chain and for all levels of supply chain planning. Advances in both operating systems and computing power make it easier and more economical to obtain this information. Information and communication technology (ICT) enables the collection, analysis, and evaluation of data and the transfer of information from one point to another. It attempts to maximise coherent messages and minimise the coupling problems between players.

All parts of the supply chain rely on ICT in the planning, operational, administrative and management processes. The customer interface can now, if required, be replaced by electronic means. Information can be used and transferred by systems, such as with demand forecasting in MRP, which can totally rely on the electronic gathering and manipulation of data.

Electronic communication can therefore enable the:
- Automatic generation of performance monitoring against pre-set key performance indicators
- Automatic tracking of vehicles, ships, airplanes (and their loads) using global positioning satellites giving constant visibility, improved safety, security and responsive routing and scheduling
- Automatic decision making e.g. stock reordering against pre-set levels and quantities Electronic Data Interchange (EDI) is the transfer of data from one computer to another by electronic means and uses agreed standards in dedicated "closed" networks. Therefore it has been replaced in many applications by "open" networks of the web and internet

The **types of data** that can be transferred are:
- Trade data e.g. quotation, purchase order
- Technical data e.g. product specifications
- Query response e.g. order progressing
- Monetary data e.g. electronic payment of invoice, electronic ticketing
- Consignment details e.g. manifests and customs details

The use of EDI in the supply chain enables a buyer to have a direct closed network link with a number of its suppliers throughout the supply chain normally referred to as a "hub". The speed and accuracy of EDI and the email/web "open" networks do contribute to shorter lead times and lower stock holding.

134

Enterprise Resource Planning (ERP); an ERP system automates the tasks of the major functional areas of an organisation,(Finance, HR, sales, production, purchasing and distribution) and stores all the data from those different areas in a single database, accessible by all.

Automatic Planning & Scheduling (APS) is generally a module of an ERP or MRP system, which gathers and analyses data on sales, purchases, production and inventory to ensure that the right materials required for the production process are always available at the right time.

Warehouse management systems (WMS) provides electronic information concurrent with goods movement and integrates physical operations with ERP systems. WMS allows for the handling of higher volumes and can also ease the transition from fixed to random storage positioning that enables more effective warehouse operations and better space utilisation.

Automatic identification of inventory is a feature of inventory management systems and facilitates the stock control through devices such as bar coding and RFID (Radio Frequency Identification). The following case study explores further RFID:

Case Study: RFID

Within the logistics industry, the potential offered by RFID appears to be generating a lively debate. On one side of the argument, some enthusiasts seem keen to portray RFID as almost a universal panacea, delivering supply chains that are characterised by 100 per cent accurate, product- level, cradle-to-grave traceability. Others, however, are highlighting a number of potential pitfalls, ranging from consumer opposition to the 'Big Brother' connotations, to doubts over current RFID technology's ability to actually meet such high expectations at a realistic cost.

Given the high profile that RFID is enjoying at the moment, it is easy to overlook the fact that this particular technology is by no means new to the logistics industry. Siemens L & A, for example, has already implemented a number of RFID-based solutions, some of which date back ten years or more. For example, in the early 1990s, a conveyor-based order picking solution created for Farnell Electronic Components used RFID tags in the tote boxes to address the poor reliability of bar code reading experienced in the company's existing order handling system. At around the same time, an REID-based system was also implemented at one of BMW's manufacturing plants in Germany. Both are still in operation today, and have been joined by a growing number of successful applications.

However, whilst RFID has been around for some time, the current level of interest is unprecedented. There are probably a number of reasons for this. In recent years, there has been an intense focus on supply chain performance, particularly amongst the major retailers. Companies have invested heavily in automated systems that improve the cost-effectiveness and efficiency of their distribution networks. In particular, the priority has been the creation of supply chains that are capable of providing each individual store with pr the quantity of goods required to its shelves. If successful, this ensures that the retailer is consistently offering customers in every one of its stores a comprehensive product range, whilst simultaneously minimising inventory levels and the need for backroom storage in retail outlets. Furthermore, to cut the time and money spent on in-store handling and shelf-stacking, retailers have sought to supply goods to stores pre-sorted (by aisle or department, for example). Over recent years, security and safety considerations have also become a much higher priority; the ability to rapidly and accurately trace and recall products is now essential, particularly where food and drink are concerned.

In many respects, the near-universal adoption of the barcode has underpinned efforts to develop this latest generation of logistics solutions. However, the demand for improved efficiency is inexorable. And whilst there may still be debate over precisely when and where it should be introduced, there can be no doubt that RFID boasts characteristics ideally suited to taking accuracy and cost-effectiveness to a higher level. Given their read/write capability, RFID tags can be reused almost indefinitely, there by eliminating the time and cost involved in printing and applying traditional barcodes. Further more, much more detailed information can be embedded within each tag. Speed and accuracy of scanning are also a major improvement on the barcode. Critically, it is possible to read simultaneously a large number of tags, without the need for line-of-sight visibility. As a result, a distribution centre can be fitted with RFID scanning 'portals' within each loading bay door to confirm the receipt/despatch of a precise stock quantity, with out any delay to material flow.

Furthermore, this process can be duplicated at any stage of the process, including, for example, inventory checks on the shop floor, or checking goods in and out of vehicle trailers equipped with a combination of GPS and RFID.

Once again, it is important to stress that such use of RFID is already a matter of fact rather than theory. In the UK, a leading food retailer is well advanced in trials of a system that replaces barcodes with RFID tags in the reusable trays used to transport chilled fresh foods from manufacturers through the distribution centres and out to the shops. Similarly, another leading supermarket chain is in the process of equipping the loading bays of its distribution centres with RFID readers.

Despite the obvious potential of RFID, it would be wrong to suggest that there are no obstacles to successful implementation. The issue of a universally accepted operating frequency has yet to be resolved.

Whilst irrelevant to closed loop systems (such as between a major retailer and dedicated suppliers), in other applications companies clearly need to be sure they opting for the 'VHS' option, rather than 'Betamax'. Furthermore, successful application of RFID demands rigorous supplier conformance. Many logistics professionals will be all too aware that this can still be a major challenge even where the humble barcode is concerned. Certain technical issues also need to be addressed. Problems can be encountered when trying to read RFID tags through water (in a pallet of frozen goods, for example). How ever, these are by no means insurmountable. More significant is the need to consider how the considerable extra volume of data that will be generated by an RFID-based system will be handled. Software is now recognised as a critical piece of the jigsaw when it comes to the creation of successful supply chain solutions and RFID will only serve to heighten this. Above all else, realising the potential benefits of speed and accuracy offered by RFID demands a WMS that is capable of genuine real-time standards of response.

These challenges notwithstanding, there can be little doubt that RFID is already established as a viable option. Certainly there is no shortage of suppliers active in the market, including globally-recognised IT consultancies and middle- ware suppliers offering wide-ranging strategic reviews and the like, but expecting some fairly steep and open-ended financial commitments in return. In reaching a decision on which supplier to opt for, companies should always bear in mind that RFID is not science fiction. Its current popularity is best seen as the latest stage in a process of evolution and development that has been taking place within the supply chain for a number of years. The era of RFID tags so cheap they are routinely applied to every product, doing away with queues at the tills and following the customer home with his or her shopping, is still a long way off.

For the moment, the benefits of this technology will be reaped in the supply chain that runs between manufacturer and DC, within the DC, and from the DC onto the shop floor. Successfully realising this potential will require a robust combination of hardware and software that can perform day- in, day-out, in the real world of distribution. Consequently, customers are likely to be best served by sup pliers whose roots lie in the logistics industry, and can demonstrate a successful record of integrating realistically-priced high technology solutions in this particular environment.

Source: SHD May 2004 www.siemens-dematic.co.uk

Computer controlled systems for storage and mechanical handling equipment (MHE), are used in storage systems (e.g. high bay warehouses and conveyors) and with remote controlled MHE.

Computerised routing and scheduling, routing of transport services can be calculated automatically according to shortest route, quickest route, or any variables chosen. Multi--drop operations can be scheduled to give the optimum sequence of pick-ups and drops according to the information provided.

Modelling; planners use computer programs to predict flows through new and modified networks and to assess proposals in terms of cost and benefit.

E-business; Electronic business refers generally to commercial transactions that are based upon the processing and transmission of digitised data, including text, sound and visual images and that are carried out over open networks (like the Internet) or closed networks that have a gateway onto an open network (Extranet). E-business is a form of EDI but it uses open, as opposed to closed, networks. Some of the E-business applications are as follows:

- Business to Business Trading Exchanges provide a two way on-line link between buyers and suppliers; they are now often referred to as a "marketplace". Suppliers can advertise their products and services through electronic catalogues; buyers can order from supplier catalogues, take part in auctions, or conduct tendering online; buyers can book travel. In industries with a large numbers of buyers and suppliers, third parties generally organise and manage such online forums. In industries with few buyers and a large number of sellers, the buyers often own and run the markets.
- Individual consumers and any system user can get up to-the-minute information, make enquiries, place orders and make payments on-line. Information about the current position and status of orders services can also be obtained.

Some examples of E-business follow:

Supply Chain aspect	Buying	Ordering	Designing products	Post sales
Information	Sharing with Suppliers	Visibility	Sharing with suppliers	Customer use records
Planning	Coordinating when to replenish	Forecast sharing/ agreements	New product launching	Service planning
Product flow	Paperless exchanges	Automated	Product changes	Automatic replacement of parts
KPIs	Compliance monitoring	Logistics track and trace	Project monitoring	Performance measurement
Business changes from "E"	On line auctions, market exchanges	Click on ordering	Mass customisation	Remote sensing and diagnostics, download upgrades

Information is required therefore for every stage of the supply chain and for all levels of supply chain planning.

All parts of the supply chain rely on ICT in the planning, operational, administrative and management processes. Information flows lubricate the supply chain, therefore using appropriate ICT is critical, the following case study looks at examples of doing this:

Case Study: Iceland, information sharing and supplier collaboration

Iceland part of the Big Food Group, is a high street supermarket chain with 760 stores across the UK and Ireland. In Iceland's 2003 annual report, it set out two strategic objectives — to develop organisation processes and people that enable efficiency and innovation; and build a reputation with suppliers as the most constructive and innovative channel to market. To achieve that, the company would have to move away from a co-managed inventory and adopt a collaborative supply chain.

Also, Iceland felt that creating a closer working relationship with suppliers would lead to efficiencies and eliminate waste within its supply chain. As such, it is one of the first retailers in Europe to allow suppliers to have visibility from the factory through to the store.

Sharing information with suppliers has dramatically increased event and promotion effectiveness, reduced distribution costs and decreased warehouse stock. Ultimately, Iceland is closer to its customers in offering the products that they want.

As a result, Iceland launched a unique collaborative initiative with many of its key suppliers. Overall, the initiative has strengthened supplier partnerships while managing the extended supply chain proactively and eliminating waste. Before this initiative, a supplier to Iceland was essentially working with limited information in an uncertain environment, resulting in markdowns or inefficient use of transport. Few suppliers had visibility beyond their despatches or knowledge of the Iceland business. When information was shared, suppliers could not react quickly enough to changes in stock requirements and increased consumer demand.

James Hulse, Iceland's supplier development manager, comments: "Suppliers rarely have sight of their products once they leave their factories, so we needed to give them a line of sight into the business. Getting forecasts wrong can and does lead to significant cases of overstock. By allowing our suppliers to get more involved in the entire supply chain, we knew we could benefit from few stock-outs, improved availability, more successful promotions and, ultimately, better customer service."

Product management
Using Portfolio Allocation and Replenishment solutions from JDA Software and innovative business practices, a number of Iceland's suppliers can now tap directly into the company's store level replenishment data to improve on-demand forecasts. Needless to say, security was paramount so Iceland developed a robust system that limited each partner's views to its own product/store level data. As a result, Iceland's suppliers are able to view only relevant data and manage their products early on — from raw material through to store level decision-making.

After running a successful pilot and training in 2003, Iceland and its chosen suppliers have accumulated a wide array of benefits. Because residual stocks, packaging and raw materials cannot necessarily be used for other products, greater supply chain visibility has been particularly beneficial for the suppliers of Iceland's own-label products, including Sun Valley Foods. Hulse says: "We are now giving our suppliers access to the store as well as warehouse data required to help them manage their business with us more effectively."

Since the introduction of the initiative, Sun Valley Foods also observed significantly lower distribution costs and increased vehicle use. This year it has achieved the lowest average pallet rate ever with Iceland. The company also boosted its confidence to improve manufacturing efficiency. Sun Valley Foods' supply chain planning manager, Ian Parkes, explains: "We try to deliver into Iceland less frequently with fuller loads, so we've reduced delivery costs significantly, partly by sharing loads with another supplier." Demand for fresh produce can now be forecasted more accurately. According to Hulse, in certain cases this has resulted in the elimination of warehouse stock that has created an additional one to two days of shelf life in store — meaning fresher produce for the consumer. Other benefits include:

- Improved service levels.
- Faster flow of product through the supply chain.
- Rational use of resources and more effective promotion planning.
- Synchronisation of production to better match supply with demand.
- Shared responsibility and mutual trust.

Building on the success of its early partners (Coca-Cola, Deans Foods, Rye Valley, Schwans and Sun Valley), Iceland's program has been progressively rolled out since June 2003 with other targeted suppliers. At least 18 suppliers are now up and running. Hulse says: "The payback has been quick which has made the investment required definitely worth it. Every supplier tells us that trading relationships have improved dramatically. And it's not just the financial return, it's also the soft benefits that everyone is talking about, such as being able to plan promotions more effectively and working more efficiently together."

Source: Logistics Manager June 2004

System Implementation

The success of any systems implementation will usually depend upon the following aspects:

Appropriate systems technology
It is necessary to identify systems technology that will fit the needs of the business now and in the future with a correct definition of objectives.

Any form of ICT should not be just a system "fix." Detailed handling and operations analysis is needed, with definite user requirements that are fully specified and agreed, followed by cost/benefit analysis of the options, with simulation if appropriate

Address all activities
Much work will be required in implementation, with investment in time to address all the operational, facilities, system and training activities. Failures often occur; because of under estimating the scale of such needed investments.

Design

The operational and the people aspects need close attention at the design stage, so the implementation is made easier. What works well here is being honest with people, sharing business objectives and explaining openly what the impacts are and not having hidden agendas. Letting people see it working elsewhere with a multi-level team, can bring forward system "champions" who then become keen to promote and sponsor the changes. Implementation is not the time to realise that users have no knowledge of the system. Software functionality is not the only requirement to be involved in implementation.

Risk/costs

Unknown factors can still arise, often due to the complexity of issues and the constant changes that may have occurred since the initial investigations to the implementation. Therefore the risks/costs need to be assessed against the planned gains/credits. All aspects of the interfaces/impacts with customers are critical aspects to be considered here. Visible top management support will be needed. Additionally a full change management programme may be required to overcome any uncertainty and anxiety.

Other effects

Beside the location of the software, there will be effects to other facilities such as new mechanical handling equipment, reconfiguring work methods, etc; as well as the requirement for user training. These all need to be considered well before the "live" date.

Project planning

Project planning with realistic timescales, needs to be internally managed with an internal project manager, who works alongside the external software provider. This will ensure that the complex details of the user's business are fully accounted for. It is the user after all, who needs to get the implementation right first time; allocation of adequate resources to undertake this is needed.

And finally

- Be prepared for things to go wrong, such as key people leaving, hardware failures and changes occurring to the normal activity. Contingency plans will be needed along with, especially, flexible mindsets and followed by responsive clear direction and action
- Testing and trialling before going live must be undertaken by users who need to subject the system to specific operational flows and activity with a clear view to bring the system "down". Learning and modifications can then be safely made and testing carried out again
- Ownership by the user is paramount as the software designers will not always be there; listening and attending to any of their issues and concerns is needed.
- Sufficient support personnel are available once the system has gone live

The consequences of poor systems implementation can be dramatic. In late 2004 two major UK blue chip companies (Sainsbury and MFI), issued profit warnings due to systems implementation problems and both specifically mentioned the supply chain as a major issue.

Therefore when appropriate ICT is not used, then the results can be dramatic, as shown by the following case study of Sainsbury:

Case Study: Sainsbury major ICT errors

1. It introduced technology too quickly
The initial timeline for Sainsbury's supply chain project was seven years, but it cut this to three years in response to a sliding share price. And instead of making an incremental switch, all hope was placed on a big-bang approach, with much of the new functionality coming on stream this summer. Other retailers have implemented more automated systems, but have taken a more gradualist approach.

2. The system did not meet expectations
The automated systems were thought to be easily capable of handling 2.5 million cases a week from around 2 000 suppliers and deliver them to more than 500 outlets every day, but they could not fill the shelves as well as the old system.
A newspaper survey of 20 Sainsbury Stores across the country published in October showed that in some Stores only 19 out of the 30 products on a shopping list of everyday items were actually n stock.

3. It chose predictive replenishment over a sales-based system
Sainsbury's just-in-time, predictive replenishment — as opposed to sales-based replenishment — was not flexible enough to cope with the many variables of food retailing. Availability levels fell below industry norms and out-of-stocks became more prevalent. Other food retailers have kept more to traditional replenishment methodologies, reluctant to take JIT beyond a certain level.

4. It followed ineffective strategies and worked 'against the market'
Sainsbury's directors have been attempting to revitalise the business for the past decade, but their share of the market has been in relentless decline. It now has a 15 per cent share of the market compared with Tesco's 30 per cent.
Other retail management teams have considered automated supply chains but decided they were too risky. Competitors have worked with the market in the implementation of new supply chains. Sainsbury's management worked against it, by or example, specifying pallet sizes that were markedly different from the industry norm.

Source: Supply Management 2 December 2004 "Digital Disaster"

Supply Chain Trends

As we have seen supply chain management is a dynamic process needing end to end visibility involving both the supply side (capacity, availability, compliance, fulfilment, and settlement); and the demand side (orders, inquiries, promotions, inventory). Additionally there are some important trends; the following attempts to demonstrate soon of these.

E-Commerce

In e-commerce, some have observed that it is the fulfilment/satisfying customer order process, that separates the e-commerce winners and losers. The following is to be considered here:

Growth of demand
- Ability to manage growing and unstable demand patterns?
- Appropriate core competence in warehousing and transport?
- Is a third party needed?
- What core competencies must be retained?
- Is the finance available to invest in the process and technology?
- Are customer relationship management (CRM) processes in place?
- Need to track and trace from order acquisition to satisfactory fulfilment (which may include a significant percentage of return)?
- Need to accept/respond to the fact that what is required today, may not be required, tomorrow

Performance quality
- Customer expectations are higher from e-commerce, such as speed and accuracy
- Customers are able to search for competitors more easily
- Customer loyalty is often related back to only the last performance/delivery
- Current internal processes need analysing:
  - What are customers needing and wanting?
  - What are the current capabilities?
  - What abilities can be added?
  - When are the required customer needs met?
  - Is support/after sales service available?

Correct technology
- Design the services required first; then explore the technology support/enabler. For example that which:
  - Compress through-put time
  - Operate in real time with radio frequency (RF)
  - Decrease bottlenecks in the processing
  - Increase "right first time" fulfilment
  - Decrease re-work/returns
  - Increase customer satisfaction
  - Decrease costs
- Technology solutions change quickly, therefore view it as a process and a means and not as an end in itself
- Do not add complexity, keep it simple and try to retain some flexibility

Supply customised products
- Customers are individuals and may need customised products/service, for example, Levi can deliver customised, made to order, jeans in 10 days
- Packing, assembly, labelling etc., to present "finished consumer products" can bring new demands to the warehousing activities

Customer returns

In many operations a high volume of return traffic has to be managed; for example, clothing catalogue companies have between 18 to 35 per cent of their delivered goods returned, whereas electrical catalogue companies report "only" 4/5 per cent returns.

This return traffic is also often referred to as 'reverse logistics' and can comprise of any of the following traffic:
- Pallets, roll-cages and other unit-load devices making the empty homeward journey
- Unwanted, damaged or defective goods being returned, for credit, replacement, or repair. In catalogue clothing for example, it is generally expected that customers do actually order goods to "try out" and that they have no intention of buying everything that they order (there is at least some degree of planning certainty for these unwanted goods).
- Products recalled due to quality or safety defects. This, however, will be more random and therefore more unpredictable than catalogue clothing.
- Used packaging being returned for re-use, recycling or for disposal as waste.

It is important to know why goods are being returned. Therefore the customer contact information and supporting technology should be adequate. Whilst some returns may be expected in overall volume terms, returns could arise due to some un-expected event; for example, the contamination of food products. These particular situations may be further complicated by police insistence on secrecy if blackmail is involved. Even if this is not the case, very often the perishable nature of the goods will have ensured that they were distributed very quickly across a large geographical area.
If goods are defective in some way that is not life-threatening, but where the consumers' reactions to the products may tarnish the company's reputation in the marketplace, then a rapid resolution of the matter may even enhance the standing of the company in the consumers' eyes.

Organising the physical return process will include transport and the "re-checking in" operations at the warehouse, ensuring that quality and condition are verified and that action is undertaken as appropriate. Isolating and quarantining returned goods can be necessary to avoid them being inadvertently dispatched again until they have been checked fully. This will be important where the reason for collection is not always immediately obvious.

Finally, there is a requirement to determine the disposal options, for example: repair, reuse, refurbish, and resale, recycle, or scrap/dispose of. There will need to be a definite policy covering these options.

UK Road network

In the UK road congestion is a major concern and the impacts of traffic congestion on journey times for freight traffic are expected to be dramatic, unless, there is fall in economic and social activity. Journeys that take longer mean more vehicles are needed to carry the same freight volumes, a simple basic point that can be easily illustrated by any transport scheduler. Road congestion can mean late arrivals, delayed deliveries, missed book in times, rejected deliveries, stock outs, lost sales and loss of customers; leading to higher costs, falls in productivity, unreliability and to that major supply chain major disrupter; uncertainty.

In recent times, road building has not keep up with the growth in road traffic and in the last 50 years, the number of cars have increased by some 15 times, whereas goods vehicles have increased by 5 times (although large good vehicles became much larger in this time). The freight industry meanwhile believes that the way forward is determine a combined transport policy aimed at encouraging motorists onto public transport, especially at peak times.
The car issue is an important one here. Brought about by improved quality of life and the personal freedom that such transport brings, car growth has been virtually exponential since the late 20th century.

As more cars are used, then more road space is used; this cause's road congestion as the extra cars need more road space but this is not provided. Less car parking space availability, due to the growth in car usage, in turn causes congestion in urban areas leading to increased freight delivery journey times with less reliability and predictability; a vicious circle that in turn leads to actually lowering the quality of life. Also the perceived "savoir" of public road transport is affected and is slowed down by the increased use of personal car transport, which then means less people use it; public transport then attracts less investment leading to an inferior availability; another vicious circle completed.

This car problem is therefore a complex one and is not a "one solution fits all" issue. In a market economy, then the price mechanism is usually brought into play, for example responses like the congestion charge in Central London.

Road capacity is determined by the speed of vehicles and the gap between them. At slow speeds, then the flow increases. But as speeds increase, then so should the gap that is left between vehicles. When traffic is free flowing, then drivers will usually widen the gap between vehicles to allow for more breaking distance. The effect of this is to lengthen the amount of road space that is occupied by each vehicle, so as vehicle speeds increase then the road capacity will decrease as fewer vehicles can fit into the space.

To illustrate this, imagine a motorway with free flowing traffic and the maximum speed for cars of 70 mph. As more vehicles join the motorway, then the speed will decrease until the road reaches its maximum designed capacity. As more vehicles continue to join, then the traffic flow becomes unstable, the speed reduces and the capacity falls until such time as it stops moving. Those who stop soon move off again, but as the following traffic is still heading into the congested area; a queue forms at the rear, whilst at the front, the traffic is accelerating away.

This is why many drivers wonder what has caused them to stop; the answer is too simple. Assuming no accident or careless driving has occurred, it is simply due to the volume of traffic that is using the motorway. Traffic has to adjust to allow vehicles to enter, which then causes knock backs to following traffic…and so it continues, often many miles back from where the traffic joins. Traffic flows are therefore dependent upon the speed of vehicles on the road and the gap between successive vehicles. Road design for single lanes with normal breaking distances, at 20 mph allows around 2000 vehicles per hour, for speeds of 50 mph, around 1400 and at 70 mph around 1100 vehicles per hour.

When designing roads therefore, the designer assumes safe speeds and safe gaps, but the fact is that drivers do not always follow these, accordingly a higher flow is actually produced. This causes motorways to be justly barely working because most of the drivers are driving unreasonably close to the vehicle in front; a dangerous situation indeed.
Little is currently being done to bring change to this critical aspect of logistics and therefore affecting all supply chain management activity.

UK Rail network

The UK rail network has a poor coverage and requires transhipment to road or to multi-modal, often at both ends of a journey. Most of the UK track network is unable to take normal continental freight gauge wagons and the network conversion is patchy and slow. There is little sign of any major investment or extension of initiatives to encourage rail freight usage in an industry made more fragmented since rail privatisation. In the market "free" economy, rail offers no viable alternative to road freight transport in the immediate future for the majority of freight that is currently carried by road.

Whether the "free" market will remain or whether some form of subsidy to move freight to rail will happen or, whether punitive measures will be taken against road traffic to force such movements, remains to be seen. Meanwhile, no doubt ad hoc and occasional schemes for rail freight may appear to be providing alternatives, however history has provided a constant reminder of this "start, stop and failure" of the rail freight "saviour," accepting of course, that history is not always a correct predictor of the future.

UK Legislation

The effect of the Work Time Directive on logistics operations (legislation introduced in April 2005), affected some companies' warehousing, distribution, logistics and supply chain strategies. This meant changes to transport operations for example, such as 2 drivers working a vehicle separately over 7 days, the use of 3 shifts in 24 hours and vehicle/trailer interchanges. The Waste Electrical and Electronic Equipment (WEEE) Directive (2002), affects anybody involved in manufacturing, selling, distributing, recycling or treating electrical and electronic equipment. Its aim is to reduce the waste arising from electrical and electronic equipment, and improve the environmental performance of those involved.

The above shows how legislation can change the ways things are done.

People Development

Competence is not a constant therefore keeping up with 'what's new' is a critical function for individuals in companies and for companies to acknowledge and therefore encourage and support peoples learning. One way to advance learning is by following a process of continuing professional development (CPD).

One definition of CPD is the systematic learning and improvement of knowledge, skills and competence throughout a professional's working life. Personal learning lies at the heart of CPD which is the method and process which uses personal power, knowledge and experience to:

- Make sense of things (by thinking)
- Make things happen (by doing)
- Bring about change (by moving from one position to another)

Learning is not a passive activity or an automatic process; it requires an active and thoughtful approach and it can be hard work. Regrettably professional development is not making good progress in the UK. In recent years, world class supply chain qualifications from the UK's Chartered Institute of Purchasing & Supply (CIPS) and the Chartered Institute of Logistics and Transport (CILT) have enjoyed their main growth from overseas in places like Africa and China. Clearly in countries like these, this reflects not only the perceived value and standard of UK supply chain qualifications but also their own national development and growth.

It seems however in the UK that there is reluctance to adequately develop professional supply chain people for the future and it seems, with a very few exceptions, that everyone prefers to leave this to someone else. Not a good sign in a changing, developing and competitive world, where development needs to be dynamic in order to keep up with factors such as rapid changes in technology, new and shifting markets and requirements for better standards faster and at a lower cost.

All these changes place emphasis on the continuing need to be professionally competent. Those who remain in the past can quickly have outdated knowledge and skills. A company only develops and learns through its people. Individuals are the constant in companies' learning and development and it is individuals who do the learning in companies. It is therefore clearly the responsibility of individuals to promote their own learning and for organisations to support this.

"World Class" supply chain management

It is useful to reflect and revise here on the key aspects of SCM and the following "10 signs" bring together aspects that must be found in any "world class" supply chain.

- Linked to and is part of the corporate strategy
- Seen as giving added value and competitive advantage to the business
- Cross functional organisational structures are found
- Information "lubricates" all the processes and the decision taking
- Key areas and performance are measured
- Lead times are checked, reviewed and evaluated, regularly
- Underpinning all decisions is "customer first" and "customer satisfaction"
- A continuous improvement culture enables people development and fosters good relationships
- External suppliers as viewed as being "integral partners" with collaboration also being found "at home" within the organisation
- Trade-off analysis is undertaken

The Supply Chain Rules

And finally as a summary, the following Supply Chain "Rules" have been noted in *"The Supply Chain in 90 minutes"* (Emmett, 2005).

Supply Chain Rule number one: "Win the home games first"
Many companies start into Supply Chain Management, by working "only," with the closest suppliers and customers. They should however, first ensure, that all of their internal operations and activities are "integrated, coordinated and controlled."

Supply Chain Rule number two: The format of inventory and where it is held is of common interest to all supply chain players and must be jointly investigated and examined
The format of inventory being raw material, sub assemblies/work in progress or finished goods. This is often held at multiple places in the supply chain and, is controlled (in theory), by many different players who are usually, working independently of each other. This results in too much inventory being held throughout the supply chain.

Supply Chain Rule number three: The optimum and the "ideal" cost/service balance will only ever be found by working and collaborating fully with all players in the Supply Chain
Full benefits of supply chain management will only come when there is an examination of all costs/service levels together with all the players. This will result in reduced lead times and improved total costs/service for all parties in the network. This means therefore, going beyond the first tier of suppliers and looking also at the supplier's supplier and so on. It represents more than data and process, it includes mutual interest, open relationships and sharing.

Supply chain Rule number four: Time is cash, cash flow is critical and so are the goods and information flows; fixed reliable lead times are more important than the length of the lead time
The importance of lead time in inventory is seen in the expression, "uncertainty is the mother of inventory." The length of lead time is of secondary importance to the variability and uncertainness in the lead time. Again, an examination of lead time throughout the supply chain, involving different players and interests, is critically needed.

Supply Chain Rule number five: The Customer is the business; it is their demand that drives the whole supply chain; finding out what Customers value and then delivering it, is critical
The customer is the reason for the business - so - continually working to serve the customer better is critical. The customer is the business, after all. But who is the customer? The traditional view is perhaps the one that has placed the order/pays the suppliers invoice, but by seeing the next person/process/operation in the chain as the customer, then, this way of thinking means that there are many supplier/customer relationships in a single supply chain. If all of these "single" relationships were being viewed as supplier/customer relationships, then the "whole" would be very different.

Supply Chain Rule number six: It is only the movement to the customer that adds the ultimate value; smooth continuous flow movements are preferable.
The movement to the customer, undertaken as quickly as possible whilst accounting for the associated cost levels, is really all that counts in adding value.

Supply Chain Rule number seven: Trade-off by looking, holistically, with all the supply chain players
There are many possibilities and opportunities available to Integrate/Coordinate/Control across the supply chain(s) networks, starting by "winning the home games first" in and between the internal functions; followed by, all of the external connections to the supply chain networks.

Supply Chain Rule number eight: Information flows lubricate the supply chain; using appropriate ICT is critical
Information is required at every stage of the supply chain and for all of the levels of supply chain planning. All parts of the supply chain rely on ICT in the planning, operational, administrative and management processes.

4.0. Action time: Electron

Electron is a global operator in the electronics market with factories all over the world. In order to compete and to ensure customer satisfaction, Electron has to manage its quality and purchasing strategy very carefully. The company recognises that customer satisfaction depends on the quality of what happens on the production line, which in turn depends on the performance of suppliers. If any of the links in the chain break down or fail to meet the required standard, then all the glossy advertising in the world is not going to make up for the customer's disappointment in a product that is unavailable, or does not work properly, or fails to meet their technical expectations.

Total quality, therefore, is an ingrained philosophy throughout Electrons' operations, resulting in better products and better processes. "Electron Quality" has five simple, but important principles:
(a) Strive for excellence
(b) Customer first
(c) Demonstrate leadership
(d) Value people
(e) Supplier partnership

Directly or indirectly, many of these principles could not be properly implemented without good relationships with the right suppliers. Philips cultivates supplier relationships based on trust and co-operation, sharing experience and expertise to benefit not only the buyer and the supplier, but also the end customer.

Together, Electron and its suppliers develop technology, solve problems, learn from experience and try to avoid errors and misunderstandings.
Clearly, Electron cannot develop and maintain deep relationships with every one of its

suppliers. Instead, it assesses its suppliers to discover which ones are the most important in terms of their strategic significance to Electrons business. These receive the most attention and investment in relationship building. Electron has three categories of supplier:

1. Supplier-partners: this might be the smallest group, but these are the most important suppliers and Electron builds intense, involved relationships with them. An important focus of the co-operation is innovation, the development of new expertise and new opportunities. These suppliers might well have essential knowledge and/or expertise that Electron could not otherwise access or develop for itself. This makes these suppliers extremely significant strategically as their loss could seriously undermine Electron current business and future direction.

2. Preferred suppliers: these suppliers are less important, but there is still good reason for Electron to work closely with them on issues such as quality, logistics and price to gain mutual benefit. The supplier does adapt itself to suit Electron requirements, to some extent, but there is not the same mutual dependence as in the first category.

3. Commercial suppliers: these are the least important suppliers and although Electron will encourage better performance in terms of quality etc, it is unlikely to get involved in helping the supplier to achieve it.

Electron also emphasises the importance of supplier revaluation as a basis for improving future performance. A supplier's actual performance is measured against mutually agreed targets in terms of quality, logistics, costs and responsiveness.

Tasks
1. Why should they go to all this trouble to develop relationships with suppliers? Why doesn't it just choose suppliers on the basis of the lowest price?
2. What do you think each of the five principles of "Electron Quality" actually means in practice? How they are consistent with the marketing concept and what impact might they have on the marketing mix?

5.0. Supply Chain Improvements

After reading this part of the book, you will better understand the following:

Performance improvements

Model for supply chain improvements
- Understand Current performance; where are we now?
- Design Improvement Strategies; where do we want to be?
- Plan New Processes and Structures; how to get there?
- Operate New Processes and Structures; do it

Performance Improvements

Throughout this book we have considered many improvements and it has often been noted that a manager has two jobs; the job they currently do and the job of improving and changing the way things are currently done.

Improving performance is therefore a fundamental aspect of management and should be a continuous process.

A set of rules for performance improvement have been seen by Balle (1997), as follows:

- Start close to the customer
- Look at the lead times
- Simplify, simplify, simplify
- Keep processes independent
- Process redesign teams are temporary
- Build a cross functional organisation
- Keep a team focus
- Top management commitment is vital

This approach is a useful overview for improving supply chain performance and as we shall see later, success will come more from people/culture change aspects than from the use of technical solutions alone.

Meanwhile, a useful starting point is process mapping.

Supply Chain Process Mapping

This analyses a supply chain by breaking it down into the component parts/processes and providing a structure for data. It acts as a lens through which to view the process and to focus the efforts on making improvement. When evaluating any business processes, it will be a usual outcome that they do not actually fully work the way which management thinks they do.

Mapping will therefore also show, how the informal system, will be different from the formally designed system. It therefore enables a better understanding and will involve questioning those, who actually work with the process. It will therefore show, "how it actually works". (We cover the "how-to" of supply chain mapping below).

Tools

After mapping then various tools can be used and the following "tool-bag" of approaches and methods can be selected as and when appropriate. It should be appreciated that tools are not a fix all solution but will only work in solving a specific problem that supports a clear direction with supporting principles.

Tools should not be separated from the thinking that is behind them, such as having a design improvement strategy, which is also covered later. We will however open this "tool-bag" here by looking at the grandparent of performance improvement; work study.

Work study

The foundation for performance improvement lies in the historic approach of Work Study, which has two main components:

1)   Method Study – How the job should be done.
2)   Work Measurement – How long the job should take.

Whilst work study is often seen as out-dated and an old approach by many; it definitely does provides a useful analytical foundational framework. In this regard, many people would argue that the "fashionable" 1990's business process re-engineering (BPR) approach is actually, method study under a new name. We look at method study next, followed by work measurement:

1) Method Study is about how the job should be done and is the systematic analysis of problems using the accepted convention and ordered sequence of "SREDIM":

- Select the area to be investigated
- Record all the relevant data on the current system
- Examine the recorded data
- Develop a more efficient method
- Install the new method
- Maintain the new method by regular appraisal

In more detail these steps involve the following:

- Selecting involves considering all the economic, technical and human factors
- Recording involves considering the use of process and flow chart diagrams, for example by using the A.S.M.E. (American Society of Mechanical Engineers) Symbols
- Examining involves using questions such as:

-   Purpose, what is achieved?
-   Person, who achieves it?
-   Sequence, when is it achieved?
-   Place, where is it achieved?
-   Means, how is it achieved?

Then asking is it:

-   Practical?
-   Economic?
-   Acceptable?
-   Safe?

The "answer" maybe in two forms, the short-term quick fix, and the longer-term solution (the ultimate objective):

-   Developing involves the Work Study Engineer, looking at the improved method from a human relations and communication viewpoint and in getting "help" in areas they will not be familiar with, e.g. cost, sources of supply, plant, quality, technology etc.
-   Installing involves reporting on findings for management approval , followed by planning the installation
-   Maintaining involves re-examining after installation:
    -   Is it living up to expectations?
    -   Are there any further changes needed?
    -   What can we learn for the future?

2) Work Measurement is about how long the job should take, and has objectives of:

-   Reducing ineffective time
-   Providing a basis for calculating the optimum work-load per person
-   Providing a basis to determine the number of people required
-   Providing standards

Techniques used include time study, using synthetic data, activity sampling, and analytical estimating. These methods involve looking at individual people doing the same work. It becomes a very detailed exercise and when it is for example, used with time study, the steps are as follows:

-   breaking a job into elements
-   applying a rating factor for each person undertaking the job
-   obtaining basic times at the standard rating of 100
-   assessing relaxation allowances on top of the standard time
-   the standard time is all the standard element times added together
-   negotiation, to arrive at the allowed time for the job

Alternatives to conducting detailed time studies are available and are as follows:

-   Synthetic data; this uses existing data from elements of jobs, for example, the predetermined average miles per hour times in the Microsoft Auto-Route programme and the results from industry benchmarking on warehouse operative pick rates.

- Activity sampling; this uses a large number of random observations to indicate the percentage of time that a different work activity occurs, within a given time period.
- Analytical estimating; this uses experience and specific job knowledge to visualise the elements needed. Next, the times are estimated in advance of the job being undertaken. Once the job has been done; then actual time is fed-back and knowledge is built up.

In summary, work study gives a very precise analytical approach, especially at the level of an individual undertaking a specific job. It provides better ways than guesswork. However, for more "combined" operations and overall processes, then other approaches to performance improvement may be used. These of course, can be very complimentary with work study. We will now look at some of these and start with method improvement.

Method improvement

As the name implies, this approach looks more at how jobs can be done better and is similar to the above mentioned SREDIM in work study and also includes process charting/mapping:

1.   Pick a job to improve
- Look for bottleneck jobs
- Jobs that take too much time
- Jobs where costs are high
- Jobs that require chasing for materials, tools, supplies
- Jobs where money can be saved
- Jobs that can be done quicker

2.   Make a process chart
- Then breakdown the job into a visual form using, for example:
    - Flow process charts : these focuses on distance
    - Multiple activity process charts : focuses on time
    - Operator process charts : focuses an individuals movements

3.   Challenge every detail
- Study for improvement
- Challenge every part of the job by asking , in order:
    - What and why?
    - Where and why?
    - When and why?
    - Who and why?
    - How and why?
- Watch for waste, like "make ready" and "put away" steps

4.   Work out a better method
- Can we eliminate unnecessary activity? (Watch especially for over transporting/ moving and storing)
- Can we combine activity? (For example, inspect "on the job")

- Can we change the sequence? (For example, eliminate back-tracking)
- Can we change the place?
- Can we change the person?
- Can we improve all the remaining aspects?
- Remember the viewpoint: "If I find a job is done the same way as it was one year ago, then I know very well it is wrong"

5. Apply the new method
- Technical problems. Will it reduce costs, increase productivity, and improve quality?
- Human problems. Remember people resist what they do not understand and people do not like being criticised. So discuss changes with those affected in advance, explain why, "sell " the change
- Test/trial, and follow through/review

Improving efficiency

This approach concentrates more towards improving the efficiency of specific operations. It also has some useful points on improvements generally:

1. Understanding the operation
- Use input/process/output diagrams
- Recognise that processes transform inputs by altering and ,or inspecting and or transporting and, or storing
- Answer the following questions: Who are the customers/what do they need/what is the product-service/what do they expect/does it meet their expectations/what process is involved/what action is needed to improve the process?

2. Set the right objectives
- Are the strategic/functional/team and personal objectives aligned?

3. Improve Work Processing
- Identify non value added/wasted time
- How can you remove it?
- Control the process by Measuring-Appraising-Acting
- Manage Risks by Appraisal (likelihood, probability, prioritise) and Contingency Planning ("what if", establish procedures, test, refine, revise)
- Improve housekeeping (for example, by using, the 5S approach of sort, straighten, sweep/shine/scrub, standardise, systemise)
- As people make the process work, so use, job enrichment and empowerment

4. Increase Capacity
- Forecast demand (using as appropriate: moving averages/regression statistical models and intuition/expert opinion)
- Plan capacity (level/fixed or variable or a mixture)
- Avoid capacity risks by changing demand and, or the resources
- Watch for the balance between, too little/too much utilisation

5. Continually improve

- Change will come from new customers/products/competitors; rising costs/falling revenues.
- Small, continual, incremental approaches do work in a culture of continual improvement. The "big bang" approach is not always needed, and when it is, then, it may be too late.
- Select an issue
- Identify the process
- Draw a flow chart
- Select an improvement measure
- Look at causes and effects
- Collect and analyse data
- Identify major causes
- Plan for improvements
- Take corrective action
- Are the objectives met?
- Write up and standardise the changes that are needed elsewhere

6. Check the customer perception

- How effective have you been?
- How can you tell?
- Ask the customer how you can improve?
- "Walk it through wearing the customers hat"
- Determinants of service are access, aesthetics, attention given, availability, care, cleanliness, comfort, commitment, communication, competence, courtesy, flexibility, friendliness, functionality, integrity, reliability, responsiveness, security

Optimising dependant processes

This approach looks more at processes that are dependant upon each other and therefore has excellent parallels with the supply chain. An overview on the approach in Balle (1997) follows:

1. Determine the Output

- Start at the customer end and establish what they do with your output
- Never ever forget, that the next link in the chain, is always the customer (whether internally or externally located)

2. Sketch the Process

- Walk through the process, collecting forms, paperwork etc
- Challenge each paper process

3. Map the process

- Establish the inputs and the outputs
- Draw the customer process
- Draw in the feedback loops
- Determine the lead times

- Time the operations
4. **Redesign the process**
- Look for bottlenecks
- Remove them one by one, thereby reducing lead time
- Concentrate on what adds value and reduces waste
- Watch for the improvement killers, such as its not possible; it's not our job; it should not be like this; the answer is obvious; I am already doing it; I will do it tomorrow etc.
- Eliminate processes and think parallel
- Split processes
- Remove unnecessary steps

5. **Test and Refine**
- Check, check and test
- Recognise limiting and restraining factors
- Expect unexpected reactions to change
- Polish the redesign

6. **Implement and standardise**
- Determine: Action/Owner/Deadline/Check/Update/Comments
- Develop best practice checklists
- Ensure that customer needs have been met

Using Questions

As Peter Drucker has noted, "The problem with western managers is the emphasis is in finding the right answer rather that asking the right question." Asking the right question first will assist to get the right answer. Clearly the above methods use questions extensively, and many more follow in the Appendix 4: Supply Chain Analysis questions.

These can be used to ensure effective performance improvements are made. They are very wide ranging and can be applied and used in many and varied ways; the following topics are covered:

- Cost Reduction
- Lead time reduction
- Quality Improvement
- Measurement systems
- Management
- Customer service
- Strategic aspects on inventory
- Demand and forecast aspects of inventory
- Lead time and methods aspects of inventory
- Warehousing aspects of inventory
- Procurement Process
- Warehousing

- Operating Freight Transport vehicles
"Cost World" and "Throughput World" improvements

We have noted earlier that cost control is only one part of an improvement process. It will also be recalled from the "Throughput World" of The Theory of Constraints (TOC) mentioned earlier, that you cannot control costs without controlling the throughput (1st) and inventory (2nd) that have caused the costs (3rd).

This leads us back to Goldratt's Theory of Constraints where the requirement to ask when making improvements is:

- What to change?
- What to change to?
- How to cause the change?

Clearly costs arise in each process and therefore, to improve costs, then we need to improve costs in each process. In Goldratt's view, this gives only a "local efficiency" in the "Cost World." To get global improvements therefore, the requirement is make many local improvements. In each process and in the supply chain, there are also throughputs. As a "chain is as strong as the weakest link" then the weak link is the blockage (or the constraint). For "global" efficiencies, then the linkages are just as important as the flow. This is Goldratt's "Throughput World." To get improvements here, we need to first change the weakest link. Improving the other links before this will result in "waste" (commented upon earlier).

As each link is dependent on the other links, then the critical path is the longest path of dependent events in time in the chain.

To summarise:

- **Cost world:** Needs local improvements with each variable link being seen as independent
- **Throughput world:** Need improvements, first, on the weakest link; with each variable link being seen as dependent on all the other links

The topic of "weak links," leads us onto another tenet in the Theory of Constraints, that of "Drum-buffer-rope". This has the underlying principle that "a system can only run as fast as the speed of its weakest link (or bottleneck)." It observes that each has a role as follows:

- The Drum beats the pace for the whole system (and the bottleneck), for example, in the supply chain, forecasts and making to stock
- A Buffer is placed in front of the bottleneck to make sure it is always worked to full capacity, for example with levels of inventory in the supply chain
- The Rope is the communication (from the bottleneck) on the rate at which material is needed at the front end of the system, for example by "push" scheduling

Traditionally therefore in the supply chain, the drum is the forecast, the buffer is the high level of safety stock and the rope is scheduling and "push methods". This in turn can mean the

following is found:
- slow responses
- potential wasted throughput
- high levels of inventory
- higher cost levels

To change this will mean altering the role of the drum/buffer/rope and this for example, will mean the:

- Drum becomes the demand and order drivers and possible resultant making to order decisions.
- Buffer becomes low to zero levels of safety stock.
- Rope becomes visibility, transparency, responsiveness and "pull methods".

In turn, this means the following will also occur:
- responding to the throughput actually needed
- holding lower levels of inventory
- lower the levels of costs
- examining trade-offs

With supply chain improvement and following the drum-buffer-rope analogy, this requires the following is undertaken:

1). Identifying the constraints, by finding the weakest link and strengthening it; e.g. physically by removing bottlenecks, e.g. by policy changes (it should be noted that policy is often the "core" problem).

2). Deciding how to fix the constraints; e.g. physically by adding capacity or, by maximising the capacity.

3). Ensuring step 2) is undertaken; e.g. by not only concentrating on the non constraints.

4). Keeping on with steps 1) and 2), until the constraint is removed.

5). After removing the prime constraint, then starting on the next one in the critical path/chain.

The Seven Wastes

The seven wastes, from Quality Management that was discussed above, are as follows:

- overproduction, for example, having excess finished goods stocks from "production only" economies of scales, especially found in "make to stock" scenarios
- waiting, for example, time spent having to queue for a machine to finish its cycle
- transporting, for example, when moving work in progress (wip) around for finishing; the transport cost is a waste and adds no value to the finished product
- inappropriate processing, for example, from over specifying/engineering
- unnecessary inventory, for example, having more stock than the required minimum

161

- needed
- unnecessary/excess motion, for example from having movement that does not contribute in getting products to customers
- defects, for example, having to correct faults and defects

Whilst originally applied and used in manufacturing for example, the "Seven Wastes" have become a "holy grail" for many improvements methods. We will therefore elaborate on them below, as you go again through the seven descriptions, it is useful to apply them to what has been said already in this book on the supply chain.

Case Study: The seven wastes

The seven wastes originated in Japan, where waste is known as "muda" and was originally developed by Toyota's Chief Engineer Taiichi Ohno as the core of the Toyota Production System (also now known as Lean Manufacturing). To eliminate waste, it is important to understand exactly what waste is and where it exists. While products significantly differ between factories, the typical wastes found in manufacturing environments are quite similar. For each waste, there is a strategy to reduce or eliminate its effect on a company, thereby improving overall performance and quality.

1. Overproduction.
Simply put, overproduction is to manufacture an item before it is actually required. Overproduction is highly costly to a manufacturing plant because it prohibits the smooth flow of materials and actually degrades quality and productivity. The Toyota Production System is also referred to as "Just in Time" (JIT) because every item is made just as it is needed. Overproduction manufacturing is referred to as "Just in Case." This creates excessive lead times, results in high storage costs, and makes it difficult to detect defects. The simple solution to overproduction is turning off the tap; this requires a lot of courage because the problems that overproduction is hiding will be revealed. The concept is to schedule and produce only what can be immediately sold and shipped, and to improve machine changeover/set-up capability.

2. Waiting
Whenever goods are not moving or being processed, the waste of waiting occurs. Typically more than 99% of a product's life in traditional batch-and-queue manufacture will be spent waiting to be processed. Much of a product's lead time is tied up in waiting for the next operation; this is usually because material flow is poor, production runs are too long, and distances between work centres are too great. Goldratt (Theory of Constraints) has stated many times that one hour lost in a bottleneck process is one hour lost to the entire factory's output, which can never be recovered ;linking processes together so that one feeds directly into the next can dramatically reduce waiting.

3. Transporting
Transporting product between processes is a cost incursion which adds no value to the product. Excessive movement and handling cause damage and are an opportunity

for quality to deteriorate. Material handlers must be used to transport the materials, resulting in another organizational cost that adds no customer value. Transportation can be difficult to reduce due to the perceived costs of moving equipment and processes closer together. Furthermore, it is often hard to determine which processes should be next to each other. Mapping product flows can make this easier to visualise.

4. Inappropriate Processing

Often termed as "using a sledgehammer to crack a nut," many organisations use expensive high precision equipment where simpler tools would be sufficient. This often results in poor plant layout because preceding or subsequent operations are located far apart. In addition they encourage high asset utilisation (over-production with minimal changeovers) in order to recover the high cost of this equipment. Toyota is famous for their use of low-cost automation, combined with immaculately maintained, often older machines. Investing in smaller, more flexible equipment where possible; creating manufacturing cells; and combining steps will greatly reduce the waste of inappropriate processing.

5. Unnecessary Inventory

Work in Progress (WIP) is a direct result of overproduction and waiting. Excess inventory tends to hide problems on the plant floor, which must be identified and resolved in order to improve operating performance. Excess inventory increases lead times, consumes productive floor space, delays the identification of problems, and inhibits communication. By achieving a seamless flow between work centres, many manufacturers have been able to improve customer service and slash inventories and their associated costs.

6. Unnecessary/Excess Motion

This waste is related to ergonomics and is seen in all instances of bending, stretching, walking, lifting, and reaching. These are also health and safety issues, which in today's litigious society are becoming more of a problem for organizations. Jobs with excessive motion should be analyzed and redesigned for improvement with the involvement of plant personnel.

7. Defects

With a direct impact to the bottom line, quality defects resulting in rework or scrap are a tremendous cost to organisations. Associated costs include quarantining inventory, re-inspecting, rescheduling, and capacity loss. In many organizations the total cost of defects is often a significant percentage of total manufacturing cost. Through employee involvement and Continuous Process Improvement (CPI), there is a huge opportunity to reduce defects at many facilities.

In the latest edition of the Lean Manufacturing classic Lean Thinking, Underutilization of Employees has been added as an eighth waste to Ohno's original seven wastes. Organisations employ their staff for their nimble fingers and strong muscles but forget they come to work everyday with a free brain. It is only by capitalising on their employees' creativity that organisations can eliminate the other seven wastes and continuously improve their performance. Many changes over recent years have driven organizations to become world class organizations or Lean Enterprises. The first step in achieving that goal is to identify and attack the seven wastes. As Toyota and other world-class organisations have come to realize, customers will pay for value added work, but never for waste.

(The above is based on an article by David McBride http://www.emsstrategies.com)

People and performance

The above discussion has shown that there are many approaches to performance improvements. The use of models is useful in as much as they can be usefully applied to a specific purpose. Additionally various aspects from different models can be used; there being no "one size fits all" model. Ultimately however, all performance improvement will involve people and a specific case study in improving people (and therefore performance) follows:

Case Study: Land Rover and people improvements in production operations

This well-known vehicle manufacturer had falling productivity and rising costs. This forced an examination of work methods.

The methods used were:
- Labour was organised into teams who were given responsibility and training in improvement methodology.
- "Work with People" was used as a theme to break down adversary relationships.
- "Everyone has two jobs-there own and improvement of their work" was another theme introduced.
- The production line was to viewed as a series of supplier/customer relationships.
- 2 hours a week was allocated to discussion groups- either internal or with external suppliers.
- Clocking in was abandoned and uniforms introduced.

Tangible results were reported as:
- Inventory fell from £23 million to £8.6 million in two years
- Output rose by 28 per cent in two years

Source: Director Magazine January 1994

The following case study also involved people to make improvements and additionally recognised that not enough effort was put into the people aspects.

Case Study: K Shoes: Changing methods of work

- Benchmarked a US Company that was using the Toyota Production System and was making shoes with fewer people with little work in progress.
- K Shoes took 150 separate operations and 12 days lead time and cut this to half a day by introducing self directed teams.
- Demand driven teams monitor sales and forecast their own production needs.
- Can now produce hundreds of different styles every week.
- Needed good communication between teams, with team leaders (who oversee 10 teams) and who meet the plant manager at least every four weeks.
- Results
  - On time delivery from 80 to 97%
  - Productivity per employee up 19%
  - Reject rates of 0.5%, fell to 250 parts per million
  - Eliminated 40 Managerial positions, for example, Quality inspectors, as quality is now everyone's responsibility. As has been said, you cannot design quality in by checking, as it is then too late.
  - Top management recognised they should have put more time into helping people understand the need for change and what options this offered

An approach to involve people and recognise improvement is called **performance management** - this is defined as "Getting results by getting the best from people and helping people achieve their potential". An extremely brief overview on how optimising performance needs to impact on people, is seen below:

Leading
- Listening to others, to understand them
- Empowering others, by giving responsibility, trust, training and support
- Adapting to changing situations
- Delivering high quality results with clear goals linked to end results
- Self understanding as the more you understand yourself and your impact on others, then, the easier it is to manage yourself and adapt your style to bring out the best in others

Coaching, delegating, motivating
- Coaching is listening, questioning and giving feedback
- Delegating is analysing a task, analysing a person, agree a monitoring system, setting the climate and reviewing progress
- Motivating involves understanding people and recognising what motivates them at different times and at different life stages

Appraising
- Performance development reviews formally, e.g. once per year, but also, continually by "Leaders" and "Coaches."

Teaming

- Team roles vary and each person has their own strengths. Teams are made effective by building on individual strengths that work towards a common goal

As mentioned, a brief coverage only of the critical aspect of people in improving performance. This has however been more fully covered in the following Improving Performance Management Toolkits by Stuart Emmett (2008):

- Systems Thinking Toolkit
- Team Toolkit
- Motivation Toolkit
- Developing People Toolkit
- Learning Toolkit
- Communication Toolkit
- Customer Service Toolkit
  and the Human Resources Toolkit by Richard McNamara (2008)

Finally in this section, the link between making technical improvements and the needed people/culture improvements is made very clear in the following case study:

Case Study: Staples USA Supply Chain Improvements

Staples USA undertook a major three-year supply chain transformation process with goals as follows:

- reduce inventory by $200 million while supporting double-digit sales growth each year.
- expand operating margins by over $100 million.
- contribute directly to sales growth through improved use of limited resources to drive demand.

To achieve these financial goals, they drove improvements in four areas:

- improved return on resource investment.
- improved measures of supply chain reliability.
- increases in effective service.
- greater coordination among supply chain participants.

Within each of these areas, over the course of three years they had over a hundred individual improvement projects.

While many of the changes made were technical in nature and involved process improvement work, the key that has unlocked dramatic value has been cultural change. Disciplined management of a transformation from a culture of safety and siloed behaviour to a culture of synchronization based on trust and teamwork has delivered a leaner more efficient and more reliable supply chain. It has also created a performance improvement culture within Staples that l lead to more improvements in economic performance and value to customers. Supply chain transformation has helped Staples deliver a combination of wins for shareholders through improved return on net assets and for customers through increased service at lower cost.

Extracted and adapted from source: Paul J. Gaffney, Executive Vice President, Supply Chain Staples, Inc. 91st Annual International Supply Management Conference May 2006

Model for Supply Chain Improvements

Throughout this book we have considered many improvements and I hope readers have been able to note and use these as appropriate.

What follows is a guiding framework and a summary of what has been earlier considered. It is not a definite step by step process that must be strictly followed. Indeed many of the steps overlap and iteration will be needed. However please, a "health warning" follows.

It seems many fundamental change initiatives fail in the UK. Look for example at the quality movement. In the 1980's this had a wide audience. By the 1990's however it was rarely heard of, apart from those companies who had succeeded. Why is this? Many reasons I guess, but one strong reason is our preference for using tools that we believe will instantly fix things. When they don't, then "quality does not work here."

We do seem to want an instant solution that is a prescriptive, "use these, then that" and because it worked for company x, then we believe it will work for us. But there likely "will be trouble ahead" as rarely will this tool-fixing be effective.

Many for example are unsuccessful with Toyota Production System (TPS) as they concentrate on the explicit tools and not on the implicit principles; they want the easy tools but not the thinking behind them.

What is first needed then is to change the thinking that has got us to where we are today so that in moving forward, we can have a better foundation and not just rely on using some "one size fits all" tools. What will also help here is to review the earlier discussion on supply chain re-thinking. After all: "The significant problems we face cannot be solved at the same level of thinking we were at when we created them." (Albert Einstein).

This will then likely involve us in doing thing differently, for example, using supported learning by doing:

- "Discovery by solving problems"
- "Discovery by asking questions"

- Changes are structured as controlled experiments
- Mistakes are allowed, this demonstrates learning
- Experiment frequently as possible
- Managers are enablers, e.g. they coach/mentor, and are not fixers

We could continue, but the aim here is to guard against seeing the Model as a "one size fits all" tool. See it please as something to guide the thinking; you may wish to consider it to be your own supply chain improvement thinking reference guide.

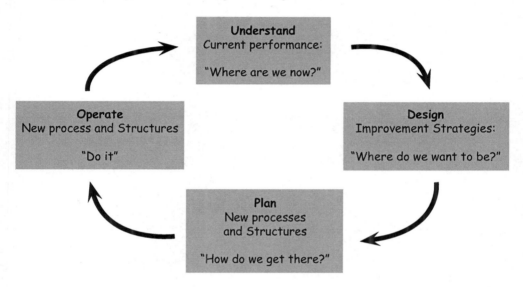

Step 1. Where are we now?

Aim: Describe the current supply chain process that exists, between your suppliers and your customers.

At this stage, do not consider any changes; only a description of how it is now.

How is the supply chain managed?
- Is it linked to and part of the corporate strategy?
- Is it seen as giving added value and competitive advantage to the business?
- What are the cross functional organisational structures?
- Will we ensure that information "lubricates" all the processes and the decision taking?
- Are key areas and performance measured?
- Are lead times checked, reviewed and evaluated, regularly?
- Does "customer first" and "customer satisfaction" underpin all decisions?
- Do we adopt a continuous improvement culture that enables people development and fosters good relationships?
- Are external suppliers viewed as being "integral partners" with collaboration also being found internally in the company?
- Is trade-off analysis undertaken?

Map the current process/inputs and outputs
- Draw the customer process; start at the customer end and establish what they do with your output. Never ever forget, that the next link in the chain is the customer. Answer the following questions:
    - who are the customers?
    - what do they need?
    - what is the product-service?
    - what do they expect?
    - does we meet their expectations?
    - what process is involved?
    - what action is needed to improve the process?
- Draw the supply process
    - who are the suppliers and the suppliers suppliers?
    - what do they need?
    - what is the product-service?
    - what do they expect?
    - does we meet their expectations?
    - what process is involved?
    - what action is needed to improve the process?
- Draw in the feedback loops

Some important aspects on how to supply chain process map are as follows:
- Doing it quickly, is better than doing it slowly
- Update regularly and often
- Use the right people (for example with the doers and the decision makers)
- Display the process on cards or post it notes/flip charts
- Walk and record the real process
- Enlist the help of people closest to the process
- Ask questions (see step 5 below)

The following five basic steps may also be used when process mapping:
1. Define that the supply chain/process to be improved
2. Identify the steps by brain storming
3. Display the process in sequence
4. Change the map to correspond to the actual physical process
5. Evaluate the process by questioning:
    - What is the purpose of?
    - Where is it done?
    - When it is it done?
    - Who does it?
    - How is done?
    - Why is it necessary?
    - Why is it done then?
    - Why does the person do it?
    - Why is it done it this way?
    - What is the lead-time?

Action time: Supply chain mapping exercise
- Mentally walk and record the processes
- Display these in sequence on the wall
- Collect ideas from a discussion
- Go through the total supply chain step-by-step
- Starting with the first operation, ask:
    - What is the purpose of this?
    - Is in this value-added?
    - Can it be eliminated?
    - If it cannot be eliminated can it be combined with another?
    - Is there are any other waste that can be eliminated?
- Repeat for all operations

Do we need to make detailed process charts for each activity?

Breakdown jobs into a visual form using, for example:
- Flow process charts : focuses on distance
- Multiple activity process charts : focuses on time
- Operator process charts : focuses an individuals movements
- Input/process/output diagrams : focuses on the connections

For each activity (for example, pre-order planning, procurement, suppliers, transit, receiving, warehouse, delivery, payment), **provide the following information:**
- Activity decision
- Frequency that activity occurs
- Who is responsible for that activity
- Information required to conduct that activity
- Average activity lead time
- Minimum activity lead time
- Maximum activity lead time
- Cause of activity lead time variability
- For the inventory, describe the types/format (RM/WIP/Finished goods) and amounts (value/quantities/days of supply) that are held.
- What KPIs do you use to assess the overall supply chain performance?

Ensure coverage of all the applicable lead times from the users need to order placement, to being finally available for issue/use by customers/consumers.

Step 2: Where do we want to be?

Aim: Design improvement strategies and challenge every detail in the current supply chain

At this stage, consider changes needed to make improvements or to take you towards the vision/future situation required.

Use the mapping exercise to improve by:
- Eliminating steps
- Performing steps in parallel
- Re-arranging steps
- Simplifying steps
- Use less expensive operations
- Use consistent operations
- Eliminating all waste and non value adders such as:
  - Time spent on correction
  - Over production
  - Inventory
  - Waiting
  - Non required processing
  - Non required movement

The minimum (but very acceptable result) that can be expected, will be lead time reductions in the processes.

Study "what can be done better" by challenging every step and asking for each step, in order:
- What and why?
- Where and why?
- When and why?
- Who and why?
- How and why?

Then:
- Check for waste, like any, "make ready" and "put away" steps
- Which steps are redundant?
- Which steps cause bottlenecks?
- Which steps add complexity?
- Which steps result in delays?
- Which steps result in storage?
- Which steps result in unnecessary movement?
- Jobs that take too much time
- Jobs where costs are high
- Jobs that require chasing for materials, tools, supplies
- Jobs where money can be saved
- Jobs that can be done quicker

Management (SCR 1; supply chain rule 1)

- Who is accountable for the horizontal cross functional end to end process performance?
- How can the company be re-structured to manage supply chain processes, in addition to the functions?
- How does what we do look and appear to the customer?

- What are the best in class indicators available?
- What is the root causes of superior performance?
- How can we better motivate job performers?

Inventory (SCR2)

Strategic aspects on inventory
- Why do you have inventory?
- What drives the present level of inventory?
- How are inventory levels set?
- How current is the decision on the inventory levels?
- How often are inventory decisions reviewed?
- What direction is inventory being driven, and why is it?
- What are the actual service requirements of customers?
- How do the direction and/or change in inventory compare with the direction and/or change in sales?
- How much of the inventory reflects safety stock?
- Who is responsible for setting and for managing inventory levels?
- Are they the same person/department or not?
- How are excess inventories, and the cost of, reflected in management responsibilities?
- How is the alternative, inventory stock outs, and the cost of, reflected in management responsibilities?
- How are ICT system algorithms and underlying assumptions reviewed?
- Is customer input used?

Lead time and methods aspects of inventory
- How variable is supplier lead times?
- How are the total lead times, including in transit stock lead times and internationally sourced items, incorporated in the system?
- How accurate are the free stock inventories that are used in the resulting production planning and sourcing?
- How is supplier reliability and lead times reflected in inventory planning and management?
- Are additional inventories factored in to buffer for each of these issues?
- How these aspects are factored into supplier selection decisions?
- Does purchasing have purchase order visibility with suppliers to control ordered items at the SKU level?
- Do suppliers understand and collaborate with the inventory philosophy and approach?
- Does purchased product flow to keep inventory in the supply chain or are they irregular, aggregated?
- How are transportation reliability and transit times reflected in inventory planning and management?
- Are additional inventories factored in to buffer for each of these issues?

Warehousing aspects of inventory
- Where is inventory stored and why?
- How many distribution centres are used and why? (Each distribution centre means additional safety stock will be carried)
- Are they in the right locations?
- How much obsolete/dead, old promotions and very slow-moving dead inventory is there?
- What is the storage cost for such "dead" inventory?
- Is inventory often transferred between distribution centres to provide inventory to fill orders? (That is inefficient use of transportation, not good customer service and resulting from wrong forecasting allocation)

Collaboration (SCR3)

Purchasing

As purchasing is central to dealing with suppliers, then we need to ensure we understand this function. The following questions will help to do this:

General Questions
- What does the Kraljic procurement portfolio tell us?
- Are quotations obtained from a number of sources?
- Are alternative suppliers approached?
- Are all purchase requisitions/purchase orders properly authorised?
- Does a policy exist for inviting bids/estimates/tenders?
- Are safeguards in existence to prevent the purchasing of excessive quantities?
- Is the purchasing department given a sound forecast of materials and other requirements in good time to enable them to be bought on favourable terms?
- Are some components currently being made that could be bought from outside at less cost?
- Ordering costs against stock-holding costs?
- Do buyers have the authority to speculate in commodity markets?

Financial questions that need to be asked
- What are the suppliers financial and credit ratings?
- What credit terms are offered?
- How do these compare with other suppliers' credit terms?
- How do they compare with the suppliers' cash flow needs?
- What are the cost implications of overdue deliveries?
- Are make or buy studies undertaken?
- Are the prices competitive (given quality levels)?
- What controls do suppliers have over their activities?
- Is standard costing employed?
- Is sufficient information available by specific cost element to know the reasonableness of the price quoted?
- Is the price reasonable in terms of competition?

- What is the supplier's current financial position as shown in the most recent balance sheet?
- What are the suppliers' current and projected levels of business?
- Are there additional sources of capital if they are needed (for the supplier)?
- What type of accounting system is employed
    - Job cost?
    - Standard cost?
    - Other?
- Price breakdowns by cost element on fixed price contracts should be furnished
- Is there any objection to contracting on other than a fixed price basis?
- Is cost accumulated by lot release, and how is initial production costs estimated?
- Is special tooling being purchased separately?
- Are there any mating/inter-changeability problems?
- Should tooling be coded?
- Have we distinguished between special tooling required for the contract and facility items?
- How are labour costs accounted for?
- Are operations covered by time standards?
- If so, how are they established?
- Are learning curves employed in projecting labour costs? If so, what rate of learning is employed?
- Are supplier's employees unionized? If so, when do union contracts expire?
- Will designated individuals in engineering, production, and finance be specified from whom the buyer can obtain pertinent in formation and data as he requires it?
- Are all necessary activities included?
- Check realistic control points and flow-times have been established
- Are loads balanced among activities so that production will proceed without delay?
- Are there any special handling, packaging or shipping requirements that may delay delivery?
- Are spares involved, and are they allowed for in the vendor's plans and schedules?
- Are all inspection, test, and engineering requirements fully understood?
- Is the item adequately described on the specification, purchase order etc?
- Are there any special test or quality control requirements the supplier must meet?
- Does he fully understand them, and does he have the time, facilities and know-how to comply?
- Are sources accustomed to manufacturing this item?
- Do they demonstrate ability to meet this schedule?
- Do their past rejection experiences demonstrate ability to meet test and quality requirements?
- Is a performance bond advisable?
- Should the IP rights be obtained to use or acquire tooling, designs, and materials to manufacture the item in case of default?
- Do we undertake TCO (Total Cost of Ownership), TAC (Total Acquisition Cost) and WLC/LCC (Whole Life/Life Cycle Costing)

Answering the above questions will help us to understand our current procurement activity; we can now more fully consider collaboration.

Why consider Collaboration?
- Where are we on the Kraljic procurement portfolio?
- Are bought in products/services more than 50% of our turnover?
- Can supplies be a source of competitive advantage?
- What are the real drivers for considering making the change?
- In 3 years, will existing suppliers be able to meet all our requirements?
- Do we need to develop new suppliers?
- Do we need suppliers that are more responsive?
- Are we prepared to be more responsive to our suppliers?
- Are we prepared to treat suppliers as partners?

Lead time reduction (SCR4)

- Which steps consume the most time?
- Why is this?
- What actions could you take to improve the lead times for Supply?
- What actions could you take to improve the lead times for Customers?
- What actions could your suppliers take to improve the lead times for Supply?
- What actions could Customers take to improve the lead times?
- What actions are needed to prevent lead time variability?
- What are your suggestions to make these actions happen?

Customer Demand (SCR5)

Establish the Key Components of Customer Service

Market research surveys identify that the top items identified (in order), are usually:
- Time to deliver ("On time")
- Reliability and "constancy" of service
- Availability of stock ("In Full")
- Advice and communication when non availability
- Quality of sales representatives/customer service department
- Product support

Identify the relative importance of each component:
- If On time, is it 2 or 3 or 4 days?
- If In Full, is it 80 or 90 or 100 per cent?

Establish "where are we now" against the importance:
- Rate current against competition by market research.

Segment the market:
- Do all customers require the same service?
- Which customers are sensitive to what specific service component?

Design the customer service package:
- Price brackets related to service levels?
- Promotions

Establish, measure and control:
- Ensure measurements are understood by all involved:
    - Order Cycle Time/On time (OT): e.g. Suppliers view maybe, despatch within 24 hours of order receipt but the Customer view is, time order placed to time received.
    - Reliability/Quality: e.g. how often 'fail', e.g. track/trace facility e.g. damage free, e.g. order convenience, e.g. documentation accuracy.
    - Accuracy/Availability/In full delivery (IF): e.g. Suppliers view maybe is to deliver 100% of what is available but the Customer view is, 100% in full order receipt.

Demand and forecast aspects of inventory
- How variable is demand?
- How is forecasting done?
- Is forecast accuracy regularly measured?
- How accurate is it, at the item/SKU level?
- How timely is it prepared and submitted?
- How does purchasing and manufacturing handle the forecast inaccuracies?
- Do they overbuy or overbuild to compensate for doubts about the forecast?
- Is inventory forecast to the distribution centre level so the right inventory at the right quantity is carried at each facility?
- Or, is the forecast at a macro level with no direction on what inventory, how much inventory and where inventory should be positioned?

Cost Reduction (SCR6)

- What does it cost to operate the processes?
- Which steps cost the most?
- Why is this?
- Which steps add value?
- Which steps do not add value?
- What are the causes of costs in this process?

Trade-offs (SCR7)

Quality Improvement
- Why do we get defects/variations?
- Is this due to common or special causes?
- What has to be managed to have the desired effect?
- How should the process be changed to reduce or eliminate defects/variations?

What impact do the current processes have?
- Why is inventory held?
- What are the inventory levels being held, downstream by suppliers and upstream, by customers?
- What adds value?
- What does not add value?
- How can we add value while reducing cost?
- Why is the process configured to run this way?
- How can the process be performed differently?
- How can we make the process more effective, efficient and flexible?
- What will the jobs in the new process consist of?
- Are we sure that we have examined all trade-off opportunities for overall supply chain benefit; for example:
  - Within activities/processes
  - Between processes and functions
  - Between functions
  - Between organisations

Information (SCR8)

Is ICT being used to enable the:
- Automatic generation of performance monitoring against pre-set key performance indicators.
- Automatic tracking of materials in vehicles, ships, airplanes using global positioning satellites giving constant visibility, improved safety, security and responsive routing and scheduling.
- Automatic decision making e.g. stock reordering against pre-set levels and quantities.

Is ICT being used to transfer:
- Trade data e.g. quotation, purchase order.
- Technical data e.g. product specifications.
- Query response e.g. order progressing.
- Monetary data e.g. electronic payment of invoice, electronic ticketing.
- Consignment details e.g. manifests and customs details.

Are the following systems being used:
- Enterprise Resource Planning (ERP).
- Automatic Planning & Scheduling (APS).
- Warehouse management systems (WMS).
- Inventory management systems (IMS).
- Bar coding and Radio Frequency Identification (RFID).
- Computer controlled systems for storage and mechanical handling equipment (MHE).
- Computerised routing and scheduling, routing of transport.
- Modelling.
- E-business applications.

Step 3: How do we get there?

Aim: Plan new processes and structures

Redesign the process
- Look for bottlenecks
- Remove then one by one, thereby reducing lead time
- Concentrate on what adds value and reduces waste
- Watch for the improvement killers = (it's not possible; it's not our job; it should not be like this; the answer is obvious; I am already doing it; I will do it tomorrow).
- Eliminate processes and think parallel
- Split processes
- Remove unnecessary steps

Increase Capacity
- Forecast demand (moving averages, regression models, intuition, expert opinion)
- Plan capacity (level/fixed or chase/variable or a mixture)
- Avoid capacity risks by changing demand and, or the resources
- Watch for the balance between the too little/too much utilisation

Work out a better method
- Can we eliminate unnecessary detail? (Watch especially for transport/movements and storage items)
- Can we combine? (For example, inspect "on the job")
- Can we change the sequence? (For example, eliminate back-tracking)
- Can we change the place?
- Can we change the person?
- Can we improve all the remaining aspects?
- Remember the viewpoint: "If I find a job is done the same way as it was one year ago, then I know very well it is wrong"

Set the right objectives
- Are strategic/functional/team and personal objectives aligned?
- Appropriate S.M.A.R.T objectives?
- Appropriate Q.C.T.D.S.M objectives?

Measurement systems
- What, from the customer expectations, are the requirements for inputs and outputs in the process?
- What should be the measured to ensure the requirements are met?
- Do the current measures assess what is important to the customers?
- What happens to the measurement data currently collected?
- Why is one measure preferable to another?
- Does the process performance data, compare to the customer expectations and perceptions?

Implement and standardise
- Determine: Action/Owner/Deadline/Check/Update/Comments
- Develop best practice checklists
- Ensure that customer needs have been met
- Manage Risks by Appraisal (likelihood, probability, prioritise) and Contingency Planning ("what ifs", establish procedures, test, refine, revise)
- Improve housekeeping (The 5S approach of sort, straighten, scrub, standardise, systemise)
- People make the process work, so use, job enrichment and empowerment

What approach will be used?
- As the changes are likely to be fundamental, what overall type of approach will be needed:
  - High level of urgency, but with low resistance; this will need a more visionary/charismatic approach
  - Crisis/low resistance; this needs a more visionary/persuasive approach
  - High urgency/high resistance; this needs a more visionary/coercive approach
  - Crisis/high resistance; this needs an autocratic, almost dictatorial approach
- Do those you wish to involve, have the ability to participate?
- Are they motivated to participate?
- Does involvement (or lack of it) fit the cultures of the organisations involved?
- How important is the post-change motivation of yours and suppliers employees?

What are the reasons for resistance?
- What threats are those affected likely to feel?
- Will there be resentment the imposed change?
- Do you understand the emotional aspects of those resisting the change?
- Do you understand the steps involved in people's behaviour during change?
- Have you considered reducing resistance by using:
  - Participation
  - Communication
  - Training

What are the impacts of making the change?
- Have you assessed the implications and effects of the change?
- Have you used force field analysis or other approaches to think through all aspects of the change?
- For the following, have you considered all aspects of the change to the organisations:
  - Tasks
  - People
  - Structure
  - Culture
  - Goodwill
  - Information systems
  - Procurement/buying process
  - Manufacturing/production process

- Distribution process
- Marketing process
- KPIs and control systems
- Reward Systems
- Have you thought through, which of the above elements have to change and how these may, in turn affect the other elements?

What are the Internal Issues?

- Will you form a multi-disciplinary project team, for example: 1 Senior Manager with Purchase - Production - Logistics - Marketing representation as well as having the appropriate and similar representation from supplier(s)
- Explore the following:
  - Consider one supply chain, or all of the supply chains?
  - Is the remit agreed and clear?
  - Who is to be involved/consulted?
  - What are the core values of the philosophy?
  - Does this fit with the current company cultures?
  - How will we evaluate suppliers?
  - What resources are needed for this programme?
  - Is a multi-functional approach valid?
  - How will effective communications be developed?
  - How will trust be developed?
  - What training is needed for our/suppliers employees?
  - Do we need a "best" supplier award?
  - How will we be consistent in practising the philosophy?
- Format an Action Plan (Written Document)
- Develop a Vision/Mission Statement, ensuring it is:
  - Credible?
  - Challenging?
  - Consistent in all parts?
  - Clear?
  - An integral part of the company cultures?
  - Providing a bridge from the past to the future?
  - Something that all project team members believe in whole-heartedly?
- Quantify Objectives
- Detail Resources & Responsibilities
- Implementation Mechanisms
- Develop a Statement of Principles
- Agree the start date
- Project team future

Get the message across:

- Have you determined how to get going?
- How to demonstrate your own belief in the vision?
- How you will use personal contact to communicate the vision?
- Whether to use workshops and conferences?

- How opportunities for two-way communication can be created?
- What communication media will be used to support the messages?
- How can you use everyday meetings to build the vision?
- The use of external public relations.
- How will you seek out and use examples of success?
- Have you thought through the detailed implementation actions to make the change happen, including:
  - Strategies to implement the vision?
  - Short-term plans and budgets to turn strategies into action plans?

Help people through:
- How will support be given to those working with you to implement the change?
- Will coaching be provided when it is needed?
- How are key people empowered?
- How will praise and thanks be given when appropriate?
- How will people be helped and assisted after making mistakes and "failing" (which are a natural part of change and of learning)?

Monitor and control the change process:
- How will you monitor and control the change process?

Key Issues about Starting Out
- Recognise you are on "A Journey to a Destination" and a process of "Courtship> Engagement > Commitment"
- Ensure internally there is:
  - understanding
  - commitment
- Recognise that the core concepts are:
  - Suppliers are seen as assets/partners
  - Internal company processes in "partnership"
  - Long term & HOT (honest-open-truthful) relationships
  - Joint views/analysis of TCO (Total Cost of Ownership), TAC (Total Acquisition Cost) and WLC/LCC (Whole Life/Life Cycle Costing)
- Anticipate problems, for example you will need:
  - more time in the early days
  - management of resources
  - "will, and all try to succeed"
  - to exchange information
  - to use open communication
  - to listen before acting
  - to receive criticism
  - to understand peoples behaviour
- Recognise that major barriers are:
  - Trust (Historical mistrust will remain until the "new" trust is formed)
  - Sharing information (Information will be seen as Power)
  - "The most powerful player is seen as wielding the big stick"

- Maybe it is better to start out by selecting a supplier/product group that will give an early and visible win/win?

And finally:
- Have you thought how you will motivate by giving recognition to those playing a part in the change process?
- Are you emotionally prepared to deal with all the unexpected things that will crop up, and all the matters you should have thought of but overlooked?
- And finally, have you:
  - A clear understanding of the change?
  - Evidence to support the need for the change?
  - Assessed the levels of support you are likely to receive from your boss and the top management of the firm?
  - Considered the value of finding a champion for the change from the ranks of top management?
  - Examined ways that you can get key managers on your side through using participation approaches?
  - Understood the dangers that face a specialist unit that is implementing change, but is otherwise isolated from the organisation?
- It is rarely easy changing "the way we have always done things around here", so do not:
  - embark on a programme lightly
  - abandon it easily
  - begin unless senior management know what could happen
  - begin unless senior management supports it fully and openly
- Ensure that you do:
  - match actions and words
  - publicise success
  - anticipate problems
  - expect eventual success

Step 4: Doing it

Aim: Operate the new processes and structures

Applying the new methods
- Technical aspects. Does it reduce costs, increase productivity, service and improve quality?
- Human aspects. Remember people resist what they do not understand and people do not like being criticised. So discuss changes with those affected in advance, explain why, and "sell" the change.

Test and Refine
- Check, check and test.
- Recognise limiting and restraining factors.

- Expect unexpected reactions to change.
- Polish the redesign.
- Follow through/review.

Check the customer perception
- How effective have you been?
- How can you tell?
- Ask the customer how you can further improve
- "Walk it through wearing the customers hat"
- Determinants of service are many, like access, aesthetics, attention given, availability, care, cleanliness, comfort, commitment, communication, competence, courtesy, flexibility, friendliness, functionality, integrity, reliability, responsiveness, security

Continually improve as:
- New customers/products/competitors and rising costs with falling revenues all means change.
- The "big bang" approach is not always needed, and when it is, then, it may be too late!
- Small, continual, incremental approaches work well where there is a culture of continual improvement.

Review the current performance
- Start again "where are we now".

5.0. Action Time: Hair Care Ltd

Hair Care Limited (HCL) is a private company and is a major supplier of hair care products to the hairdressing trade. Their products are well liked by professional hairdressers and the company enjoys a good share of the market.

HCL has not, until recently, contemplated the supply of products to the retail market, but an enquiry from a major national multiple has led to the supply of samples and to the consumer testing of a HCL shampoo.

The outcome of the trial shows that many consumers prefer the HCL shampoo and discussions have now moved to the possibility of HCL becoming a regular supplier. It is envisaged that products will be shipped in large quantities to the retailer's RDCs, branded as the retailer's own product.

The HCL management team is attracted to the idea; it would enable them to expand their production and sales without the need to spend any money on marketing and, without the need to worry about setting up a distribution system. If the project is successful, it might also lead to the launch of the HCL brand through the retail trade and possibly to contracts with other major retailers for own brand products. HCL has been having discussions with Trade Pack, their present supplier of shampoo bottles. These are of one litre capacity, to a standard design and are supplied in plain white. HCL then applies the label for their small range of trade products.

Trade Pack is also excited by the possible new business that HCL diversification will bring. They will be very happy to invest in the necessary tooling to produce blow-moulded bottles in large quantities to a design specified by HCL and its retail customer.

However, problems are emerging. Trade Pack's plant is 200 miles from HCL and shipping large quantities of shampoo bottles means shipping large volumes of fresh air. The cost of packaging is also a large proportion of the cost of producing small bottles of shampoo.

There are local suppliers who could supply at a lower and feasible cost but HCL have never dealt with them and, in any case, they have a sense of loyalty to Trade Pack.

After a brainstorming session, the management of HCL has come up with the following possibilities. They have not, yet, paid any attention to the feasibility or appropriateness of any of them:
- Re-source the bottles locally, saying thank you but goodbye to Trade Pack.
- Invest in moulding machinery, hire the appropriate expertise and integrate bottle production with their filling line, i.e. become bottle makers.
- Invite Trade Pack to set up a small plant nearby.
- Suggest that Trade Pack set up a filling line and HCL will ship shampoo in bulk to their site for filling and distribution.
- Propose a joint venture with Trade Pack, sharing resources, investment, profits, worry and everything else.
- Request the assistance of the retailer in managing part of their supply chain.
- The list is not a complete set of possibilities and some of the ideas on the list are not necessarily mutually exclusive.

Tasks:

1. Conduct and evaluate a supply chain audit of the current operation

2. Design improvements.

3. Determine an optimum supply chain solution for HCL.

4. Devise a suitable implementation plan for your solution.

Appendix one: Abbreviations

ABC	activity based costing
ABC	the 80/20 rule or Pareto analysis (often called ABC analysis)
ADC	automated data collection
ATO	assemble to order
BPR	business processing re-engineering
CMI	co-managed inventory
CPFR	collaborative planning forecasting replenishment
DPP	direct product profitability
ECT	efficient consumer response
EDI	electronic data interchange
EVA	economic value added
FG	finished goods
GPS	global positioning satellite
FMS	fast, medium, slow
HOT	honest, open, truthful
ICT	information communication technology
IT	information technology
ID	identification
JIT	just in time
KPI	key performance indicator
LCC	life cycle costs
LT	lead time
LTV	lead time variability
MHE	mechanical handling equipment
MTO	make to order
MTS	make to stock
NDC	national distribution centre
OTIF	on time in full
PCC	primary consolidation centre
QA	quality assurance
QC	quality control
R&D	research and development
RDC	regional distribution centre
RM	raw materials
RF	radio frequency
RFID	radio frequency identification
ROCE	return on capital employed
ROI	return on investment
SCM	supply chain management
SCR	supply chain rule
SKU	stock keeping unit
SLT	supply lead time

SLTV   supply lead time variability
TAC   total acquisition costs
TOC   theory of constraints
TCO   total cost of ownership
TQM   total quality management
WMS   warehouse management system
VMI   vendor managed inventory
WEEE   waste electrical and electronic equipment
WIP   work in progress
WLC   whole life costs

Appendix two: Further information

Institutes

- Chartered Institute of Logistics and Transport: www.ciltuk.org.uk.
- Chartered Institute of Purchasing and Supply: www.cips.org
  (There are also hundreds of links available from the above sites)

Journals/Magazines

- Focus, magazine of Chartered Institute of Logistics and Transport: www.ciltuk.org.uk.
- Handling & Storage Solutions: www.western-bp.co.uk
- Health & Safety (HSM): www.western-bp.co.uk
- Industrial Handling & Storage: www.dmgworldmedia.com
- International Journal of Logistics Research and Applications:www.tandf.co.uk/journals
- Logistics Business: www.logisiticsbusiness.com
- Logistics Europe: www.logisticse.com
- Logistics Manager: www.centaur.co.uk
- Materials Handling News (MHN): www.nexusmedia.com
- Motor Transport: www.reedbusiness.co.uk
- Storage Handling and Distribution (SHD): www.turret-rai.co.uk
- Supply Management: magazine of Chartered Institute of Purchasing and Supply: www.cips.org
- Supply Chain Business: www.supplychainbusiness.com
- Warehouse News: www.warehousenews.co.uk

Appendix three: Supply Chain Analysis Questions

These questions can be used to ensure effective performance improvements are made. They are very wide ranging and can be applied and used in many and varied ways.

The following topics are covered:
- Cost Reduction
- Lead time reduction
- Quality Improvement
- Measurement systems
- Management
- Customer service aspects
- Strategic aspects on inventory
- Demand and forecast aspects of inventory
- Lead time and methods aspects of inventory
- Warehousing aspects of inventory
- Procurement Process
- Warehousing
- Operating Freight Transport vehicles

Cost Reduction:
- What does it cost to operate the process?
- Which steps cost the most?
- Why is this?
- Which steps add value?
- Which steps do not add value?
- What are the causes of costs in this process?

Lead time reduction:
- Which steps consume the most time?
- Why is this?
- Which steps add value?
- Which steps do not add value?
- Which steps are redundant?
- Which steps cause bottlenecks?
- Which steps add complexity?
- Which steps result in delays?
- Which steps result in storage?
- Which steps result in unnecessary movement?

Quality Improvement:
- Why do we get defects/variations?
- Is this due to common or special causes?

- What has to be managed to have the desired effect?
- How should the process be changed to reduce or eliminate defects/variations?
- Is there a culture of continuous improvement?

Measurement systems

- What, from the customer expectations, are the requirements for inputs and outputs in the process?
- What should be the measured to ensure the requirements are met?
- Do the current measures assess what is important to the customers?
- What happens to the measurement data currently collected?
- Why is one measure preferable to another?
- Does the process performance data, compare to the customer expectations and perceptions?

Management

- Who is accountable for the horizontal cross functional end-to-end process performance?
- How can the company be re-structured to manage processes, in addition to the functions?
- How does what we do, look and appear to the customer?
- What are the best in class indicators available?
- What is the root causes of superior performance?
- Why is the process configured to run this way?
- How can the process be performed differently?
- How can we make the process more effective, efficient and flexible?
- How can we add value while reducing cost?
- What will the jobs in the new process consist of?
- How can we better motivate job performers?
- Is every manager dedicated to creating an environment in which every employee is motivated and happy?

Customer service aspects

- How well do we deliver what we promise?
- How often do we do things right the first time?
- How often do we do things right on time?
- How quickly do we respond to requests for service?
- How accessible are we when customers need to contact us?
- How helpful and polite are we?
- How well do we speak the customer's language?
- How hard do you think we work at keeping customers a satisfied client?
- How much confidence do customers have in our products or services?
- How well do we understand and try to meet customers special needs and requests?
- Overall, how would customers rate the appearance of our facilities, products and people?
- How willing would customers be to recommend us?
- How willing would customers be to buy from us again?

Strategic aspects on inventory

- Why do you have inventory?
- What drives the present level of inventory?
- How are inventory levels set?
- How current is the decision on the inventory levels?
- How often are inventory decisions reviewed?
- What direction is inventory being driven, and why is it?
- What are the actual service requirements of customers?
- How do the direction and/or change in inventory compare with the direction and/or change in sales?
- How much of the inventory reflects safety stock?
- Who is responsible for setting and for managing inventory levels?
- Are they the same person/department or not?
- How are excess inventories, and the cost of, reflected in management responsibilities?
- How is the alternative, inventory stock outs, and the cost of, reflected in management responsibilities?
- How are ICT system algorithms and underlying assumptions reviewed?
- Is customer input used?

Demand and forecast aspects of inventory

- How variable is demand?
- How is forecasting done?
- Is forecast accuracy regularly measured?
- How accurate is it, at the item/SKU level?
- How timely is it prepared and submitted?
- How does purchasing and manufacturing handle the forecast inaccuracies?
- Do they overbuy or overbuild to compensate for doubts about the forecast?
- Is inventory forecast to the distribution centre level so the right inventory at the right quantity is carried at each facility?
- Or, is the forecast at a macro level with no direction on what inventory, how much inventory and where inventory should be positioned?

Lead time and methods aspects of inventory

- How variable is supplier lead times?
- How are the total lead times, including in transit stock lead times and internationally sourced items, incorporated in the system?
- How accurate are the free stock inventories that are used in the resulting production planning and sourcing?
- How is supplier reliability and lead times reflected in inventory planning and management?
- Are additional inventories factored in to buffer for each of these issues?
- How these aspects are factored into supplier selection decisions?
- Does purchasing have purchase order visibility with suppliers to control ordered items at the SKU level?
- Do suppliers understand and collaborate with the inventory philosophy and approach?

- Do purchased products flow to keep inventory in the supply chain or are they irregular, aggregated?
- How are transportation reliability and transit times reflected in inventory planning and management?
- Are additional inventories factored in to buffer for each of these issues?

Warehousing aspects of inventory
- Where is inventory stored and why?
- How many distribution centres are used and why? (Each distribution centre means additional safety stock will be carried)
- Are they in the right locations?
- How much obsolete/dead, old promotions and very slow-moving dead inventory is there?
- What is the storage cost for such "dead" inventory?
- Is inventory often transferred between distribution centres to provide inventory to fill orders? (That is inefficient use of transportation, not good customer service and resulting from wrong forecasting allocation)

Procurement Process
- What are the annual spend and requirements of the purchasing portfolios?
- Is there a programme to reduce the procurement lead times?
- Is component variety limited by looking closely at users specifications (avoiding brand names), and duplicated purchasing
- What are the supplier assessment methods and supplier management policies?
- What codification is used?
- Is end to end product evaluation used by applying the total costs of ownership (TCO)?
- What programme is there to develop relationships with users/customers and with external suppliers
- Have buyers changed from being reactive order placers to be proactive commodity managers?
- Should you outsource or manage procurement yourself?
- Is there a programme to reduce the supplier base to a small number of qualified suppliers fully integrated into the business?
- Are alternative suppliers approached?
- Are quotations obtained from a number of sources?
- Are all purchase requisitions/purchase orders properly authorised?
- Does a policy exist for inviting bids/estimates/tenders?
- Are safeguards in existence to prevent the procurement of excessive quantities?
- Is the procurement department given a sound forecast of materials and other requirements in good time to enable them to be bought on favourable terms?
- What are the ordering costs against stock-holding costs?
- Do buyers have the authority to speculate in commodity markets?
- What are the cost implications of overdue deliveries?
- Is sufficient information available by specific cost element to know the reasonableness of the price quoted?

- Is the price reasonable in terms of competition?
- What is the supplier's current financial position as shown in their most recent balance sheet?
- What are the suppliers' current and projected levels of business?
- Are price breakdowns by cost element on fixed price contracts furnished?
- Will designated individuals in the suppliers' organisation be specified from whom the buyer can obtain relevant information and data?
- Are there any special handling, packaging or shipping requirements that may delay delivery?
- Are spares allowed for in the supplier's plans and schedules?

Warehousing
- Are the warehouses viewed as a critical step in the material flow cycle or as a necessary evil?
- Is there a high regard for the customer?
- Do we know the customer requirements?
- Do we consistently meet these requirements?
- Are warehouse standards established?
- Is performance measured against these standards?
- Are timely actions taken to overcome any deviations?
- Are systems and procedures put into effect that will allow proactive planning of operations as opposed to reactively responding to external circumstances?
- Have we examined the trend towards larger, centralised warehouses instead of smaller, decentralised warehouses?
- Do we make use of third party public warehouses to handle peaks will be in commonplace?
- Do we appreciate that the reduction of lead times, shorter products lives, and increased inventory turnover will result in an increase in the pace of the warehouse?
- Do we appreciate that different SKU's and additional special customer requirements will result in an increase in the variety of tasks performed in the warehouse?
- Are all warehouse systems, equipment and people flexible?
- What do we minimise uncertainty?
- Are all activities within the warehouse (receiving, storing, picking and delivery) integrated within the overall material flow cycle?
- Is cycle counting used to manage inventory accuracy with accuracy above 95 per cent?
- Is space used efficiently and effectively?
- Is quality housekeeping a priority and a source of employee pride?
- Is the critically of order picking understood?
- Are procedures and layouts designed to maximise picking efficiency and effectiveness.
- Are suppliers, customers, and the functions within the warehouse integrated into a single service-providing facility?
- Are automatic identification systems the norm for data acquisition and transfer?
- Do we use real time, paperless control systems throughout the warehouse?

Operating Freight Transport vehicles
- Are our service levels reliable?

- Do we give "value for money" cost/service performance?
- How do we know?
- Do we monitor properly vehicle fuel efficiency per vehicle and per driver?
- What actions do we take on poor performance?
- Do we monitor properly vehicle turnaround times?
- What actions do we take on poor performance?
- Are our drivers and staff, friendly and approachable?
- Do we have a clean and tidy appearance of vehicles, premises, drivers and staff?
- Do we offer consignment tracking and instant POD information availability?
- Can we easily respond to special requests and requirements?
- Do conducts safe and secure operations and follow all the appropriate legislation?

Bibliography

Anderson & Lilliecreutz: *The Challenge in Supply Chain Innovation*. 2003. 19th Annual IMP Conf., Sept. 2003, Lugano.

Balle. *The Business Process Re-engineering Toolkit*. 1997. Kogan Page.

Balle. *Systems Thinking*. 1994. McGraw Hill.

Bell. S. Letter in *"Management Today"*. March 2004.

Best Factory Awards. 2001.

Cox *et al*: *Logistics Europe*. June 2002.

Director Magazine. January 1994.

Emmett S: *Getting the people right in ILT Focus*. April 2003

Emmett S. *Excellence in Warehouse Management*. 2005. Wiley.

Emmett S. *The Supply Chain in 90 Minutes*. 2005. Management Books.

Emmett S & Crocker B. *The Relationship Driven Supply Chain-creating a culture of collaboration*. 2006. Gower.

Emmett S: *Logistics Freight Transport*. 2006. Cambridge Academic.

Emmett S & Granville D. *Excellence in Inventory Management*. 2007. Cambridge Academic.

Emmett S. *The Improving Performance toolkits*. 2008.

Gaffney, Paul J. *Staples USA and Transformational Supply Chain Performance Improvement* taken from the 91st Annual International Supply Management Conference May 2006.

Goldratt E. *The Goal*. 2003. Gower.

IBM. *Follow the leaders*.

International Freighting Weekly. 27 February 2000.

Logistics Manager. Import Logistics. January/February. 1998.

Logistics Manager. Procurement Survey. June 2003.

Logistics Manager. June 2004. Collaboration and Proctor and Gamble Logistics Manager.

Logistics Manager.. March 2005. Wolseley.

Michaels L. Letter in *Management Today.* March 2004.

Motor Transport. 29 August 2002. New Look.

Motor Transport. 20 October 2002. Dunlop and Goodyear.

Motor Transport. 27 March 2003. Halfords.

Motor Transport .17 July 2003. Reverse logistics.

Partnerships with People. Department of Trade & Industry. 1997.

Porter M. *Gaining Competitive Advantage.* 1985. Free Press.

PRT & MC *Managing Supply Chains in 21st century.*

Rethinking Construction. 1998.

Signals of Performance. The Performance Measurement Group, Volume 4. Number 2 - 2003.

"Strategic Alliances: How to Make 1+1=3". Michael Patton at ISM 91st Conference May 2006.

Supply Management. 9 April 1998. Import logistics.

Supply Management. 20 April 2000. Lead times at B&Q.

Supply Management. 19 June 2000. NHS.

Supply Management. 29 June 2000. Outsourcing.

Supply Management. 2 December 2004. Digital disasters.

Supply Management. 18 January 2007.

Sunday Times, 11 February 2007.

SHD. December 2002. UK Manufacturing supply chains.

SHD. May 2004. RFID.

The Audit Commission, *Fruitful Partnership.*

Index